75. n

ANCIENT MONUMENTS OF KASHMIR

ANCIENT MONUMENTS
OF KASHMIR

BY

RAM CHANDRA KAK

FORMERLY DIRECTOR OF THE DEPARTMENT OF ARCHÆOLOGY AND
RESEARCH, JAMMU AND KASHMIR STATE

WITH A FOREWORD BY

LIEUT.-COLONEL SIR FRANCIS YOUNGHUSBAND,
K.C.S.I., K.C.I.E.

AND AN INTRODUCTION BY

PROFESSOR A. FOUCHER

ORIGINALLY PUBLISHED IN 1933 BY
THE INDIA SOCIETY,
3, VICTORIA STREET LONDON. S.W.I.

SAGAR PUBLICATIONS
18, INDIAN OIL BHAWAN, NEW JANPATH MARKET
NEW DELHI-1.

REPRINTED IN INDIA IN 1971
AT THE OXFORD PRINTCRAFT INDIA PRIVATE LTD., NEW DELHI
AND PUBLISHED BY N. K. SAGAR, FOR SAGAR PUBLICATIONS
18, INDIAN OIL BHAWAN, NEW JANPATH MARKET, NEW DELHI

FOREWORD

KASHMIR is renowned throughout the world for its beauty—for the girdle of snowy mountains which surround the lovely Valley, for its rivers and lakes and its primeval forests, and for its moderate temperature. To the dwellers in the heated plains of India it has therefore ever been a paradise of bliss. Who that has heard of it has not pined to go there? Who that has once visited it has not pined to go there again? Who that has gone there again has not wished to remain there for ever?

To the great ones of India it has always had an attraction, and where great ones go there much remains. Such marks remain in Kashmir. But they need study for their understanding and this study is now being more and more made. The latest is this present book, in which we are informed of the wonderful monuments of ancient times still standing in the beautiful Valley.

We are indebted to His Highness the Maharaja of Jammu and Kashmir, who gave the necessary permission and financial help for this valuable book to be published by the Society. It has been written by my friend Pandit Ram Chandra Kak, the recent Director of Archæology to the State. We are very grateful to Professor Foucher for having written an introduction.

FRANCIS YOUNGHUSBAND.

January 24, 1933.

TABLE OF CONTENTS

[The list of abbreviations used in footnotes will be found on page xvi.]

LIST OF ILLUSTRATIONS

INTRODUCTION

NOT all the people who visit Kashmir go there only to hunt, or to fish or to dance. Some take with them to the Happy Valley interests of a more intellectual kind, and for them the India Society has had the excellent idea of publishing this volume by Mr. Ram Chandra Kak. Such travellers are more numerous than one might expect; and from my own experience I can guess how welcome to them will be this Guide to the Ancient Monuments of Kashmir: I know how delighted I should have been on my first visit to find such a guide already made, instead of having to improvise one for myself, one much less accurate and much less complete. Not only this: the many plates accompanying the volume will serve to remind the returned traveller of the beauty of Kashmiri sites and buildings, and to the intending traveller will give food for his imagination. No very long experience is needed to teach one that dreaming before and remembering after are the best parts of travelling.

The format is handy. Condensed into 170 pages the reader will find all the general information he can reasonably desire on the geography, history, architecture and archæology of Kashmir. May we venture to regret (specialists are never satisfied) the absence in this first edition of a paragraph (which the author is eminently fitted to supply) on the popular customs and beliefs still surviving in the Valley under the official veneer of Brahmanism or Islam? No doubt these matters crop up accidentally here and there in the course of the book. But tourists would find much interest and " inspiration "— as an American would say—in hearing what the Kashmiri peasants have to tell concerning the genii, elves, and fairies with which their land abounds. What familiar echoes would arise in their memories

at tales of the Nagas who dwell at the bottom of springs and lakes in
wonderful palaces; of the Pisachas, those wicked little demons who
have so long made the Valley uninhabitable for men in the winter;
and of the Yoginis who on summer nights, like the Mænads of old,
are heard hooting on the mountain tops! And how could the
traveller, as he goes rambling about, fail to be impressed and intrigued
by the mystery of those " natural images " which show the features of
some divinity in the lines of a rock or a cliff; by the solitary chanting
of the old priest who, in his rustic shrine, celebrates the rites of bygone
days; or by the common sight of people on the bank of a stream,
offering their sacrifices in honour of the *manes* of their ancestors?
For here the visitor is no longer in India, a land closed to strangers.
All through the summer the Kashmiris live in the open air; at every
step one meets with superstitions and local customs; one lives, as
it were, in the very midst of folklore, and ceremonies to which
it would be hard to gain access in the peninsula are here visible to
all eyes.

May I go further and say what I believe to be the true reason for
this special charm of Kashmir, the charm which everybody feels, even
those who do not try to analyse it? It cannot be only because of its
magnificent woods, the pure limpidity of its lakes, the splendour
of its snowy mountain tops, or the happy murmur of its myriad brooks
sounding in the cool soft air. Nor can it be only the grace or majesty
of its ancient buildings, though the ruins of Martand rise at the prow
of their *karewa* as proudly as a Greek temple on a promontory, and the
little shrine of Payar, carved out of ten stones, has the perfect proportions of the choragic monument of Lysicrates. One cannot even
say that it comes of the combination of art and landscape, for fine
buildings in a romantic setting are to be found in many other countries.
But what is found in Kashmir alone is the grouping of these two
kinds of beauty in the midst of a nature still animated with a mysterious life, which knows how to whisper close to our ear and make the
pagan depths of us quiver, which leads us back, consciously or un-

consciously, to those past days lamented by the poet, when the world was young, when

"le ciel sur la terre
Marchait et respirait dans un peuple de dieux."

Personally, I have often thought that there remains more classic antiquity still living in the shadowy heart of the Kashmiri jungle than in the theatrical scenery of the Mediterranean shores.   Here, too, vines hang from the trees; Gujar shepherds play upon their pipes at the foot of the pine trees, just like the Sicilian shepherds in Theocritus; at eventide pious hands place small clay lamps on the rims of tutelary fountains, and make libations of milk and offerings of flowers to them as once were made to the Naiads; so much so that one might expect to espy through the deep thicket "the satyrs' dancing which imitates Alphesibœus."   For it is not true that great Pan is dead: that is only a rumour which he spread so that they would cease to pursue and persecute him.   Chased out of Arcady, the Kashmir of Greece, he found a last retreat in the lost valleys of the Himalayas, whither Dionysos, when he took him to the conquest of India, had taught him the way.

But a mystic fancy leads me astray.   No doubt we should do better to remain on the solid ground of archæology and let ourselves be led by our author from temple to temple, from mosque to mosque, from Mughal garden to Mughal garden, round Srinagar, or up or down stream.   On all these remains of a glorious past he has much information to give us, no less judicious than accurate.   Therefore no Indianist can help regretting that the local Archæological Survey—directed for ten years (1919-29) by Mr. Kak, whose success is attested by the improved state of preservation of the buildings, and by the well-catalogued collections in the Sri Pratap Singh Museum of Srinagar—was so shortlived, and that the State felt obliged to make use of the young archæologist's activities in more modern directions. His researches had already begun to throw light on the obscure period of Kashmir art before the sixth century A.D.   And the India

Society does a great service to our studies by giving him this opportunity of publishing (pl. 15-42) the curious results of his excavations at Harvan.   The multifarious reliefs on these terracotta tiles, together with the few stucco heads picked up at Ushkar (pl. 58), not only have much to tell about the barbarian invaders of India in the first century A.D.; they now supply a bond (by the intermediate links of the finds made at Taxila, Gandhara and Hadda) between the Kashmir antiquities and those of Kapisa and the valley of Bamiyan.

In conclusion, may we say that what surprises us most in this book is that its author is a pure Kashmiri ?   To those who knew—or from the writings of Sir Aurel Stein, their last patron, know—the type of the old *pandits*, nothing could be more unexpected.   These *literati* were, to be sure, excellent people, and admirably versed in their Sanskrit texts, but they were devoid of historical sense and their intellectual horizon was bounded by the narrow limits of their native Valley.   It seems almost miraculous that, after a single generation, one of their descendants is able to write in English a work so impartial and so judicially critical on the antiquities of his country.   But the miracle is explained—let us add this to spare the author's personal modesty—first by the exceptional intellectual qualities of the race; then by the excellent teaching now offered at the Government College of Srinagar, affiliated to the Panjab University; and lastly by the five years of archæological training (1914-19), which Mr. R. C. Kak spent in India under the incomparable direction of Sir John Marshall.

A. FOUCHER.

PREFACE

THE volume of literature dealing with Kashmir is very large. Indeed, almost every one who comes to Kashmir—the number of visitors is legion—and who possesses the gift of stringing words together, feels impelled to write a book, or at any rate a series of articles, on what is called "The Happy Valley." There would therefore be no justification for the present writer to add to the plethora of books on an oft-traversed subject, were it not for the fact that there is no information available in a handy, compact, and easily accessible form on the ancient monuments of Kashmir. Though several valuable accounts have been published of the various classes of monuments in the valley, they are mostly scattered over Journals of learned Societies, Archæological Survey Reports, and other similar publications, to which the general reader has not easy access. The present volume therefore needs no apology.

The book has been planned to suit the convenience and the requirements of the visitor who, without desiring any great erudition, takes an intelligent interest in the subject of Archæology. The monuments are grouped, not according to their age or style, but in regard to their situation, so that the visitor may complete his inspection of the monuments in one district before he starts for another.

The chapter on Harwan excavations is comparatively profusely illustrated, the reason being that this is the first time, save for a short notice in the *Illustrated London News* in December, 1925, that an illustrated account of those excavations has been published. They were carried out by the present writer when in charge of the Archæological Department of Jammu and Kashmir. The funds for this work, as well as for all other archæological operations in the State, were generously provided by the Government of H.H. the Maharajah of Jammu and Kashmir.

R. C. KAK.

LIST OF ABBREVIATIONS USED IN FOOTNOTES

A.S.R.	=Archæological Survey of India Reports.
Bernier	=*Travels in the Mughal Empire*, by François Bernier, edited by Vincent Smith.
Fergusson	=*History of Indian and Eastern Architecture*, by James Fergusson, 1910 ed.
J.A.S.B.	=*Journal of the Asiatic Society of Bengal*.
J.B.B.R.A.S.	=*Journal of the Bombay Branch of the Royal Asiatic Society*.
J.R.A.S.	=*Journal of the Royal Asiatic Society of Great Britain and Ireland*.
Rajat	=*Rajatarangini* of Kalhana, translated by Sir Aurel Stein (Constable).
Vigne	=Vigne's travels.

ANCIENT MONUMENTS OF KASHMIR

I

INTRODUCTION

THE COUNTRY AND ITS PEOPLE

KASHMIR proper is an irregularly oval valley 84 miles long from north-east to south-west by 20 to 25 miles broad. Its height above the sea level is everywhere over 5,000 feet. It is enclosed on all sides by ranges of snow-capped mountains, which vary at different points from 12,000 to 18,000 feet in height. The correctness of the local tradition regarding its lacustrine origin in remote prehistoric times has been demonstrated by the discovery of marine fossils and other characteristic features in the surrounding mountains and uplands. Politically it was, ordinarily, limited to its geographical frontiers, the mountain ramparts; but the neighbouring hill principalities of Prunts (Poonch) and Rajauri were often within its sphere of influence. The extent of that influence usually depended upon the personality of the ruler for the time being. Some of its more energetic kings extended their sway to the north and north-west of the Panjab, and one king, Lalitaditya (in the middle of the eighth century), is credited with having effected the conquest of Kanauj.

The valley itself was divided into two great territorial divisions, Madavarajya, the southern half, and Kramarajya, the northern half; Srinagar, the capital, was included in the former. Madavarajya, modern Maraz, is represented by the present-day *wazarat* or district of Anantnag, and Kramarajya by the *wazarat* of Baramula. The large lateral valleys drained by the Sindh and the Lidar formed integral parts of their respective districts. The two rural divisions were in

I

their turn subdivided into smaller areas—known in later times as *parganas*—which consisted of groups of villages ranging in number from a dozen to perhaps a hundred or more. The capital, though forming part of Maraz, practically constituted an independent unit; and owing to its situation at the point of contact of the two main divisions, its compactness, the presence of the court, its large population, its organised public opinion, and the superior culture of its inhabitants, it was the most important of all. Its alliance or opposition almost always proved a decisive factor in determining the fortunes of war. Its position in the centre of a large, fertile, and populous valley, intersected by navigable rivers, canals and lakes, not only made it a point of vantage commercially, but also sufficiently accounts for the failure of all the attempts made from time to time to remove it from its present position to some other place.

The most striking features of the Kashmir landscape are its mighty mountain ramparts, its beautiful lakes and rivers (Plates I and II), and its dry brown *karewas*. The former have largely determined the political fortunes of the little country they encircle. It is the inaccessibility and practical impregnability of these natural defences rather than the valour of Kashmiri troops that has so often turned the tide of invasion from the valley, when far more powerful kingdoms succumbed to it. This inaccessibility, again, enabled Kashmir to preserve and consolidate its peculiar social and economic conditions up to very recent times. While, thus, the mountains long served as effectual barriers against foreign invasion, and as a sure means of conservation of indigenous culture, they do not appear to have proved equally effectual in preventing natives of the valley from seeing something of the world which lay beyond their circumscribed horizon. Kashmir played a notable part in the propagation of Buddhism in foreign lands, especially in China and Tibet. We may mention a single instance.[1] Kumarajiva's distinguished scholarly labours in China during the régime of the later Chin dynasty (A.D. 384-417) gained for him the title of

---

[1] Gemmell, *Diamond Sutra*, p. x *et seq.*

Tungsheo, which interpreted means that "although young in years he was ripe in the wisdom and virtues of old age." He is referred to as "one of the four suns of Buddhism," and is credited with the introduction of a new alphabet. In mediæval times when, according to the great Muslim scholar Alberuni, Kashmir had closed her gates to intercourse with foreign lands, her pandits lived as honoured guests at the courts of Indian princes; for instance, Bilhana, the well-known author of the *Vikramankadevacharita*, was the court poet of Vikramaditya VI (A.D. 1075-1126) of Kalyana in Southern India (modern Kalyani in the Nizam's Dominions). The numerous rivers and lakes, besides being invaluable as commercial waterways and producers of a variety of much prized foodstuffs, have from time immemorial been the means of innocent and inexpensive pleasure to the people. The former, specially the Vitasta, the largest of them all, have also been important in the physical history of the valley. Indeed, with the exception of the uplands commonly called *wudars* or *karewas*, which date back to the lacustrine epoch, the whole of the valley owes its formation to deposits of river alluvium. This deposition of silt is still in progress, and consequently the level of the low-lying parts of the valley, particularly those where the Vitasta, carrying the drainage of the whole valley, debouches into the Wular lake, is year by year being slowly but steadily raised. According to Brahman tradition, every lake and river and spring of the valley has a divine origin and a sacred mission to fulfil—viz., washing away the sins of the faithful. The Vitasta is, above all, the sacred river, and is said to contain within its waters all that is holy in the world. Indeed Kashmir itself is considered to be the holiest of all the holy lands; it is called the Rishibhumi, "the land of sages," Śaradapitha, "the eternally pure seat of the goddess Śarada." It has not only its own Prayaga[1] (the Vitasta corresponding to the Jumna and the Sindh to the Ganges) and its own

---

[1] The confluence of the Ganges and the Jumna at Allahabad is called Prayaga. Among the Hindus it is held to be one of the holiest places of pilgrimage.

Kurukshetra,[1] but it has also the replica of almost every other important river or spring that is held in reverence in India.

The uplands or *wudars*, officially known as *karewas*, range in height from 100 to 300 feet and in area from 5 or 6 square miles to over 50 square miles each. With one or two exceptions they are dependent for their productivity upon rainfall. In ancient times, when the population of the country was probably much larger than at present, not only these *wudars*, which are still for the most part under cultivation, but also the comparatively high mountain slopes, were cultivated, as is evidenced by the existence to this day of innumerable terraces surrounded and supported by cyclopean walls at Pandrethan, Avantipur, and almost everywhere. The chief crop and, therefore, the staple food of Kashmir is rice; though maize, barley, and wheat are sown in unirrigated uplands.

With the exception of a few Sikhs and Rajputs who have settled here during the last century, the whole of the valley is occupied by Kashmiri-speaking people, who are linguistically, and perhaps ethnologically also, distinct not only from the Indians of the plains, but also from Gujars, Khakhas, and Bombas, who inhabit the neighbouring hills. The substratum of their language, after its Sanskrit superstructure has been removed, appears to be akin to Dardic, which under various names and forms is spoken by the Kanjutis of Hunza and Nagar, Kafirs of the Karakoram, and other tribes inhabiting the great mountain barrier which separates North-western India from Central Asia.

The comparative immunity from fear of foreign domination, due to the strength of the country's natural defences and to the practical impregnability of the routes leading to it, the abundance and variety of wholesome and nutritious food, the mild and salubrious climate, the narrowness of the geographical horizon—the Kashmiri could see his whole world from the roof of his house—are largely responsible for

---

[1] Near Delhi. The great battle celebrated in the Indian epic of Mahabharata was fought here.

moulding the character of the inhabitants of the Happy Valley, a character which has remained unaltered for many centuries.

SOURCES OF KASHMIR HISTORY.[1]

Our knowledge of the political, social, and economic conditions which prevailed in early Kashmir is exceptionally ample, and is derived from a variety of sources. References to the country and its people are found in the literature of the Greeks, the Chinese, and the Arabs, as well as in Indian literature. Incomparably the most authoritative and informative are, naturally, the indigenous writers of Kashmir.

GREEK NOTICES.—Speaking of the geographical position of the country, which he calls by the name of Kaspeiria, Ptolemy remarks that it is situated " below the sources of the Bidaspes (Vitasta) and of the Sandabal (Chandrabhaga) and of the Adris (Iravati)." He further states that it lies between the Daradrai or Darads on the Indus and Kylindrine or the land of the Kulindas on the Hyphasis (Bias) and eastwards. His definition of its territorial limits is considerably exaggerated.

The passage in the *Bassarika* of Dionysios of Samos, preserved by Stephanos of Byzantium, which makes mention of the Kaspeiroi as a tribe famous among the Indians for their fleetness of foot, probably refers to the Kashmiris, whose marching powers, owing to the mountainous nature of their country, are greater than those of the Indians of the plains.

CHINESE NOTICES.—The information which the Chinese records have left us is much more ample. The earliest reference which can with certainty be attributed to Kashmir is dated A.D. 541. It describes the northern part of India as a country " enveloped on all sides like a precious jewel by the snowy mountains, with a valley in the south which leads up to it and serves as the gate of the kingdom." But by

[1] This section is mainly derived from Sir Aurel Stein, *Rajatarangini*, translation, vol. ii, pp. 351-385.

far the greatest Chinese authority on Kashmir is the pilgrim Hsüan-tsang, who visited Kashmir in A.D. 631 and spent two years there studying "the Sutras and Śastras."

A fairly detailed description of the country is contained in the itinerary and life of Hsüan-tsang, who was accorded a princely welcome by the ruler of Kashmir. He entered Kashmir by way of Baramula. He found Buddhism flourishing though not predominant. On his nearing the capital the king came out to receive him, and invited him to a sumptuous feast at the palace. He gave him twenty scribes to copy the sacred books and Śastras, and also deputed five men to wait on him and to furnish him, free of expenses, with whatever he required.[1]

Speaking of the state of learning in Kashmir, he says that "this country from remote times was distinguished for learning, and their priests were all of high religious merit and conspicuous virtue as well as marked talent and power of clear exposition of doctrine; and though the other priests (i.e., of other nations) were in their own way distinguished, yet they could not be compared with these, so different were they from the ordinary class."[2]

Regarding the extent of the country, its products, and its people, he says that "it (Kashmir) was above 7,000 li (1,400 miles) in circuit, surrounded by high steep mountains over which were narrow, difficult passes, and the country had been always impregnable. The capital, which had a large river on its west side, was 12 or 13 li (about 2½ miles) from north to south and 4 or 5 li (nearly a mile) from east to west. The district was a good agricultural one and produced abundant fruits and flowers; it yielded also horses of the dragon stock, saffron, and medicinal plants. The climate was very cold in season with much snow and little wind. The people wear serge and cotton (pai-tieh). They were volatile and timid; being protected by a dragon they crowed over their neighbours; they were good-looking, but deceitful; they were fond of learning and had a faith which embraced orthodoxy and

[1] Beal, Life of Hiuen Tsiang, p. 69.   [2] Ibid., p. 71.

heterodoxy (*i.e.*, Buddhism and other religions). Buddhist monasteries were above 100 in number, and there were 5,000 Buddhist brethren; and there were four Asoka topes each containing above a pint (*shêng*) of the bodily relics of the Buddha."[1]

The territories of Prunts and Rajauri were at the time of Hsüan-tsang's visit subject to the king of Kashmir.

The next Chinese pilgrim who has left us an account of Kashmir is Ou-k'ong, who reached Kashmir in 759 A.D. Here he took his full vows as a regular monk. He resided in the country for four years, spending his time mainly in visiting holy places and in studying Sanskrit. He states that the number of Buddhist convents was more than three hundred; which shows that Buddhism was in a much more flourishing condition than in the preceding century when Hsüan-tsang visited Kashmir.

A somewhat earlier and more interesting reference is furnished by the annals of the T'ang dynasty of China. "These mention the arrival at the imperial court of the first embassy from Kashmir sent by king Tchen-t'o-lo-pi-li (in or shortly after A.D. 713), and that of another embassy sent by his brother and successor, Mu-to-pi."[2] These kings are to be identified with Chandrapida and Muktapida-Lalitaditya mentioned in the *Rajatarangini*. Besides the information that Hsüan-tsang gives, the only item of interest that this account furnishes is a reference to the Mo-ho-to-mo-loung or Mahapadma lake (present Wular lake), Po-lo-ou-lo-po-lo, Pravarapura, the old and official name of Srinagar, and Mi-na-si-to, the Vitasta river, which flowed on the west of the capital.

From this last statement, as well as from the testimony of Hsüan-tsang, it may be inferred that in the seventh and eighth centuries the city of Srinagar lay only on the right bank of the river and had not yet extended to the left bank. This expansion must have taken place some time before the end of the tenth century A.D., as Alberuni

[1] Watters, *On Yuan Chwang*, vol. i, p. 261.
[2] *Rajat.*, vol. ii, p. 357.

(see below) speaks of the city being situated on both banks of the river.

ARAB NOTICES.—The above is practically all that the Chinese have to tell us about Kashmir. The next foreigner from whom we get information of real value is Alberuni, the great Muhammadan scholar who flourished at the court of Mahmud of Ghazni (A.D. 996-1031). He tells us that, owing to the victories of Mahmud over the Hindus, the Hindu sciences have retired far away from those parts of the country conquered by us and have fled to places where our hand cannot yet reach—Kashmir, Benares, and other places.

Notwithstanding the numerous difficulties which the contemporary political conditions of India placed in the way of his collecting accurate statistics of the remote valley, Alberuni seems to have succeeded in the attempt better than might have been expected; for his account of Kashmir is much fuller than that of other parts of India and appears to show that among his informants, if not among his actual teachers, there were Kashmiri scholars.[1] Regarding the people and the country he remarks as follows:

The inhabitants of Kashmir are pedestrians, and they have no riding animals. The nobles among them ride in palankins called *kati* carried on the shoulders of men. They are especially anxious about the natural strength of the country, and therefore take always great care to keep a strong hold upon the entrances and routes leading into it. In consequence it is very difficult to trade with them. In former times they used to allow one or two foreigners, particularly Jews, to enter their country; but at present they do not allow any Hindu, whom they do not know personally, to enter, much less other people.

The best known entrance to Kashmir is from the town Babrahan (in the district of Hazara). . . . The city of Kashmir covers a space of four *farsakh*, being built along both banks of the river Jailam, which are connected with each other by bridges and ferry-boats.

[1] *Op. cit.*, vol. ii, p. 359.

He adds that four *farsakh* below Addisthan, the capital, is a swamp of one square *farsakh*: that the people have plantations on its borders, and that Kashmir has no Varshakala (rainy season), but a snow-fall beginning with Magh up to the middle of Chaitra, when continual rains set in.[1]

Kashmir holds the same rank among holy places as Benares, Kurukshetra, etc.

" The second of the month of Chaitra is a festival to the people of Kashmir called *Agdus*, and celebrated on account of a victory gained by their king Muttai over the Turks."[2]

Alberuni counts five days' march " to the beginning of the ravine whence the river Jailam comes "—that is, to the entrance of the gorge through which the river flows immediately below Baramula. This estimate agrees closely with the actual road distance between Muzafferabad and Baramula, which is given by Mr. Drew as 84 miles. At the other or Kashmir end of the ravine, Alberuni places quite correctly the watch station Dvar (Skr. Dvara), the position of which, as we shall see below, is marked to this day by the site of the old gate known as Drang.

" Thence leaving the ravine you enter the plain, and reach in two

[1] Alberuni's *India*, translated by Sachau, vol. i, p. i, p. 206 *f.*

[2] *Op. cit.*, vol. ii, pp. 178 *et seq. Agdus* mentioned here may possibly be a mispronunciation of Okduh, which in Kashmiri means the first day of a lunar fortnight. Assuming this to be correct, the difficulty as to how Alberuni could confound the first day of the month or of the fortnight with the second day still remains, unless we further surmise that the festival day went under the same name. Modern Kashmir affords several interesting parallels of this case. Thus the Kashmiri pandits celebrate their Shivaratri " Herath " festival on the thirteenth day of the dark half of Phalguna ; but that does not prevent them from speaking of Heratsa tsodah, which means the fourteenth day of Herath, which itself is celebrated on the thirteenth. A closer parallel is that of the Mahanavami. This term means " the great ninth day " and is given to two famous festival days. But one often hears such expressions as " Mahanava-hanz-pantsam," " Mahanavam-hanz-tsoram," which if literally interpreted would mean " the fifth day of the great ninth day," " the fourth day of the great ninth day," while their actual meaning is the fifth or the fourth day of the fortnight on the ninth of which the Mahanavami festival is to be celebrated.

more days Addishtan, the capital of Kashmir, passing on the road the village Ushkara." All this is perfectly accurate. Adhisthana, the capital, is, of course, meant for Srinagara, and Ushkara for Ushkur opposite Baramula, the ancient Hushkapura already mentioned by Hsüan-tsang. Alberuni's mention of Ushkur, which is on the left river bank, shows that then as now the ordinary road from the "Gate of Varahamula" to Srinagar passed on the left or southern side of the valley. Two marches are still counted for this part of the journey.[1]

"Marching on the right side (of the river), you pass through villages, one close to the other, south of the capital, and thence you reach the mountain Kularjak, which is like a cupola, similar to the mountain Dunbawand (Damawand). The snow there never melts. It is always visible from the region of Takeshar and Lauhawar (Lahore)."[2]

Besides describing the valley with great accuracy, Alberuni makes mention of the adjacent hill territories of Bolor (Baltistan) and the Dard tracts of "Gilgit, Aswira, and Shiltas" (modern Gilgit, Hasor, and Chilas). He also speaks of the fortresses of Lauhur (Skr. Lohara), in the Loharin valley on the way to Poonch, and Rajagiri as the strongest places he had ever seen.

He closes his account with a reference to the town of Rajavari (Skr. Rajapuri), the modern Rajauri. In Hindu times it was the capital of a small hill state, situated immediately to the south of the Pir Pantsal range and often tributary to Kashmir. Alberuni distinctly names it as the farthest place to which the Muhammadan merchants of his time traded, and beyond which they never passed.[3]

INDIAN NOTICES.—The information that we can glean regarding Kashmir from the works of ancient Indian writers other than those of Kashmiri origin is extremely meagre. The great grammarian Panini and his commentator Patanjali make a bare mention of the

[1] *Rajat.*, vol. ii, p. 362.   [2] *Op. cit.*, p. 363.
[3] *Op. cit.*, p. 364.

name *Kasmīra* and its derivative *Kāśmīra*. The *Mahabharata* and the *Puranas* refer to the Kāsmīras and their ruler, but in a fashion so general and vague that nothing but the situation of the country in the hill region to the north can be concluded therefrom.[1]

Varahamihira, the well-known Indian astronomer, who probably lived about A.D. 500, had even more hazy notions regarding the location of Kashmir, inasmuch as he mentions it along with a number of purely mythical countries and people such as " the kingdom of the dead " (Nastarajya), " the gold region," " the one-footed people," etc. His mention of Abhisaras, Daradas, etc., who were undoubtedly living on the borders of Kashmir, does not help much in gaining knowledge of the valley as it existed at that time.

" Perhaps the most specific piece of information regarding Kashmir that Sanskrit literature outside the valley can furnish is conveyed in the term *kāśmīra* or *kāśmīraja*, which designates the saffron, and also, according to the lexicographers, the root of the *kustha*, or *Costus speciosus*. As both saffron and *kustha* have been from early times famous products of Kashmir, the origin of the term is clear enough."[2]

KASHMIRI AUTHORS.—In strong contrast to the lack of definite geographical knowledge displayed by Indian authors is the refreshing abundance of historical and topographical detail in the works of Kashmiri authors. This splendid array of authoritative guides begins with the *Nilamatapurana* and continues practically without break to the present time. The age of the *Nilamata* is uncertain; but there is evidence to show that in one form or the other it was extant in the early middle ages. Beginning with the legend regarding the lacustrine origin of the valley and its drainage after the death of Jalodbhava, the water demon, who infested the lake and made human habitation on its shores impossible, the Purana gives us a detailed list of the holy places of Kashmir. To each name it appends a more or less comprehensive topographical description, which is of great value in identification of the numerous places mentioned.

---

[1] *Op. cit.*, p. 365.   [2] *Op. cit.*, p. 365.

Analogous in nature, but far later in date, are the *Mahatmyas* of the different *tirthas* or places of pilgrimage. These works give lengthy accounts of the legendary origin of the holy places of Kashmir, and the religious merit accruing to the fortunate pilgrim who pays a visit to each sacred spot. They also furnish a complete survey of the sacred places of Kashmir.

By far the greatest amount of our information regarding ancient and mediæval Kashmir is supplied by indigenous historians, of whom Kalhana is the oldest and most informative. He composed his *Rajatarangini*, the river of kings, in A.D. 1148-49. Born in a Brahman official family, and learned in the traditions of his country both from oral and written sources, Kalhana was specially fitted for his self-imposed task, which he has executed with conspicuous ability. His father, Champaka, was the minister of king Harsha (A.D. 1089-1101), but after the murder of his master in A.D. 1101 neither father nor son appears to have taken office under the succeeding rulers. With the characteristic reticence of ancient Indian authors he has left no information regarding his own life and pursuits. The indirect evidence of his chronicle, however, compensates to some extent for his silence by revealing the character and intellectual equipment of the man. He had a keen, observant eye, considerable sense of humour, vivid poetic imagination, and extensive knowledge of human nature. His impartiality in according praise or blame to his royal contemporaries, no less than to the kings of the past, shows that he was no sycophant. Though by birth he was a worshipper of Śiva, he respected other sects and religions almost as much as he did his own form of faith. His appreciation of the material conditions of his country, his topographical detail, his use of archæological and numismatic evidence in the compilation of his history, give his work not only an absorbing interest in itself, but also an honourable place among histories of the mediæval world.

It has, however, shortcomings which cannot be ignored. His chief defect is his want of critical acumen. He seldom quotes an opinion or a statement with a view to refute it. He is not able to distinguish between the legendary and genuine elements of tradition. Owing partly to this defect and partly, probably, to want of authentic sources, the first four books of his chronicles are little more than dynastic lists, interspersed here and there with anecdotes. It is from the seventh century A.D. that history in the modern sense begins. This does not mean that the earlier part of the chronicle is on that account without interest. On the contrary, it has very great value, not only because it mentions the great historic names of Asoka, Kanishka, etc., but also because it presents us with a fairly detailed account of the general condition of the kingdom before we reach the centuries which immediately precede the time of Kalhana, and for which he had genuine oral and written information. The latter consisted of a number of ancient histories written before Kalhana's time, of which he appears to have made extensive use. Unfortunately all of them are now lost. This makes it impossible to distinguish what is original from what is borrowed in Kalhana's *Rajatarangini*. Perhaps this work, which probably served as a convenient and comprehensive manual of Kashmir history for subsequent generations, was not a little responsible for the gradual disuse and final disappearance of the literary records which were available in his time. The period which he knew personally or the knowledge of which he owed to living witnesses is treated by him with an exhaustiveness which leaves little to be desired, especially when we bear in mind that Kalhana regarded himself primarily as a poet, and composed the *Rajatarangini* as a didactic poem for the edification of his countrymen. Kalhana's chronicle has been published, with an excellent translation, exhaustive introduction, numerous explanatory notes, and a valuable monograph on the ancient geography and coinage, etc., of Kashmir, by Sir Aurel Stein. This monumental work is indispensable for the proper understanding of the social and political conditions of pre-Muslim Kashmir.

Exactly three centuries passed before a successor was found to continue Kalhana's work. He was another Kashmiri Brahman,

Jonaraja, who was the contemporary and court historian of Zain-ul-abidin (A.D. 1421-1472).   His treatment of the centuries between him and his great predecessor is very superficial.   The greater part of his work as well as of the history of Srivara, his pupil, who continued his master's task, is devoted to the reign of their patron Zain-ul-abidin. Prajyabhatta and Suka, two other historians who followed Srivara, bridge another century and terminate their labours with the conquest of the valley by Akbar in A.D. 1587.

Thenceforward, Sanskrit chronicles ceased to be written; for, though Akbar tolerated and even encouraged Sanskrit learning, in such an out-of-the-way place as Kashmir it was no doubt at a discount, at any rate in an official sense.   But with the decay of Sanskrit learning the Kashmiris' characteristic love of history and tradition did not wane and wither away.

Before bidding farewell to our Kashmiri Sanskrit writers, we must make mention of the poets from whose works can be gleaned some useful information.   The most important among them is Kshemendra, the well-known historian, whose books, composed in the second and third quarter of the eleventh century, form important landmarks in several fields of Indian literature.   In the *Samayamatrika*, one of his most original poems, which is intended to describe the snares of courtesans, he gives us, among other stories, an amusing account of the wanderings of his chief heroine, Kankali, through the length and breadth of Kashmir.   The numerous places which form the scene of her exploits can all easily enough be traced on the map.   More than once curious touches of true local colour impart additional interest to these references.   To Kshemendra's poem we owe, for example, the earliest mention of the Pir Pantsal pass (Panchaladhara) and its hospice (*matha*).   There too we get a glimpse of the ancient salt trade which until lately continued to follow that route.[1]

Bilhana, the poet, who has been alluded to above, has also left in his *Vikramankadevacharita* a glowing picture of the beauties of Kashmir

[1] *Op. cit.*, p. 375.

in general, besides giving a description of his rural home at Khuna-musha, which is known today as the rakh (game preserve) of Khunamoh.

Mankha, the contemporary of Kalhana, has left a similar description of Kashmir and Srinagar.

These accounts serve the additional purpose of enabling us to corroborate the statements of Kalhana from independent evidence.

The book known as the *Lokaprakaśa* is a curious mixture of the ordinary dictionary and a practical handbook dealing with various topics of administration and private life in Kashmir. Though much of the information given in it is decidedly old and probably from the hand of our well-known Kshemendra, there are unmistakable proofs in the form and contents of the book that it has undergone considerable alterations and additions down even to the seventeenth century. It supplies the earliest list of Kashmir parganas; and there are also the names of numerous localities inserted in the forms for bonds, *hundis*, contracts, official reports, and the like, which form the bulk of *Prakaśas* ii and iv.[1]

In Mughal times and later, a host of Muslim and Hindu historians writing in the official Persian language recorded the events that occurred in their own lifetime, as well as the traditions which they heard from living witnesses. None of them, however, reached the standard of Kalhana. What little they tell of the Hindu period they borrowed from him, and borrowed in a most perfunctory manner. The most important among these later historians are Haidar Malik of Tsodur, a contemporary of the emperor Jahangir; Narayan Kaul, who compiled his history in A.D. 1721; Hasan, who wrote in the last quarter of the eighteenth century; and Birbal Katsur, who is still more recent.

Besides the indigenous Sanskrit and Persian chronicles, we have notices of foreigners who collected information or visited Kashmir from time to time and recorded what they heard, or saw with their own eyes. Of these Mirza Haidar Doghlat of Kashgar, who conquered the valley in A.D. 1540 and ruled it in the name of Humayun till A.D. 1551,

[1] *Op. cit.*, p. 376.

the historian Firishta, and Abul Fazl, the minister of Akbar, are the most instructive. Abul Fazl's account is specially interesting. Besides supplying detailed information regarding the administration of the country, its products and industries, it furnishes an account of its chief places and objects of note, a list of thirty-eight parganas or administrative divisions with their respective land revenue figures in kind and in cash, and of the tribes residing in each. It also furnishes a short résumé of the history of Kashmir, which Abul Fazl had got summarised from indigenous sources.

Among the European travellers who visited Kashmir before the valley became the fashionable summer resort of India, the earliest to contribute to our knowledge of it is the French physician Bernier, who accompanied Aurangzeb in his journey to Srinagar in A.D. 1664. He has left many interesting descriptions of the " merveilles," as he calls them, of Kashmir, as well as of the general condition of the country in Aurangzeb's time. The travels of Foster afford a peep into the state of tyranny that prevailed in the valley during the Pathan régime. Moorcroft, Vigne, Hügel, Honigberger, and Jacquemont are valuable for the Sikh times.

In addition to the numerous sources of Kashmir history above mentioned, we have to take into account the extraordinarily tenacious oral traditions, which have been handed down from generation to generation. They remove uncertainty in the identification of many ancient names given in the chronicles, and in certain cases they supplement the information furnished.

II

POLITICAL HISTORY[1]

THE nature and extent of the information on ancient Kashmir which can be gleaned from the accounts of foreign writers have been already indicated. It remains to give a brief outline of its history from the detailed narratives of the Kashmir chroniclers.

Of the long line of royal figures which fill the first three books of Kalhana's *Rajatarangini* we know little more than the names. The only kings whose existence is corroborated by contemporary historical records of India are Asoka, the great Buddhist emperor of India (272-232 B.C.), Kanishka and Huvishka, the Kushan kings of Gandhara, whose sway extended from Patna to Kashgar and Yarkand (second century A.D.), and Toramana and Mihirakula, the White Hun invaders who devastated Northern India in the fifth century A.D. It is interesting to observe that these great rulers, of whose possessions Kashmir formed only a small part, appear in Kalhana's chronicles as mere local rajas who had, in certain cases, extended their conquests abroad. His attempts at arriving at their respective dates are hopelessly confused and entirely at variance with the accepted chronology of India; but the tradition from which he derived his information was substantially correct in its description of the general character of their administration.

In Pravarasena II, who seems to have flourished some time in the later half of the sixth century, there appears, for the first time, a purely indigenous ruler possessing a truly historical character; but it is with the accession to the throne of the plebeian Karkota dynasty, about the middle of the seventh century A.D., that the authentic history of Kashmir begins. Considerations of space forbid inclusion of an account,

[1] This chapter was originally published with slight variations in the *Journal of Indian History*.

however brief, of every ruler who filled the throne of Kashmir for the next five centuries (the period for which Kalhana is our guide). A few names, those of Lalitaditya, Jayapida, Avantivarman, queen Didda, Sussala and Jayasimha, stand out among a crowd of petty princelings, the majority of whom did little to earn the gratitude or merit the remembrance of posterity.

PRAVARASENA II.—Among the kings of Kashmir who preceded the Karkota dynasty, Pravarasena II is easily the most prominent. He seems to have spent the earlier portion of his life in exile, while the kingdom of his fathers was being ruled by Matrigupta, a foreigner and a nominee of king Vikramaditya of Ujjain. Legend credits him with extensive conquests in Northern India and the replacement of Śiladitya-Pratapaśila of Malwa (circa A.D. 580) on his throne. But the chief historical interest of his reign is centred in his foundation of the city of Srinagar. He named it Pravarapura, a name which is still current among the learned, but the younger city soon assumed the name, as it had already usurped the dignity, of the old capital of Asoka, which has since been called Puranadhishtana, modern Pandrethan, 3 miles above Srinagar. The new city can be proved to have occupied its present site, and seems to have enjoyed an uncommon degree of prosperity during the reign of its founder, as can be gathered from the poetic description of Kalhana, who states that " the city was once famous as containing 36 lakhs of houses. It was provided with regularly arranged markets and was at first only on the right bank of the Vitasta." " There are mansions which reach to the sky and ascending which one sees the earth, glistening in the rain at the close of the summer and covered with flowers in [the month of] Chaitra."

LALITADITYA-MUKTAPIDA.—About a century and a half elapsed before another great and truly historical figure occupied the Kashmir throne. This was Lalitaditya-Muktapida, who succeeded his vicious, short-lived brother, Tarapida, and reigned gloriously for thirty-six years, about the middle of the eighth century A.D. He was by far the most heroic ruler that Kashmir had ever produced. Popular tradition, still living, credits him with immense conquests, stretching in India from shore to shore, and extending beyond the snowy mountain barrier to the parched "ocean of sand" in Central Asia. His march into Hindustan seems to have been more of a military raid than a permanent occupation of the country. Thus he swooped with his army upon Kanyakubja, modern Kanauj, and before king Yaśovarman of Kanauj had probably time to recover from the surprise, his army was annihilated and he found himself reduced to the necessity of suing for an ignominious peace. His further conquests bear a legendary character; but the fact of his sending an embassy to the Chinese court, as stated by the T'ang annals, seems to show that he knew something of the power of that empire by actual experience. It is, however, chiefly through his unstinted patronage of the arts and sciences, his erection of a number of magnificent buildings, and his wise, though by no means mild, administration of the country, that Lalitaditya lives in the memory of posterity.

Among the towns that he founded, the chief are Parnotsa, the capital of the modern territory of Poonch and still a flourishing town, Lalitapura, and Parihasapura, both of which have dwindled into petty hamlets. The last named he chose as his capital in preference to the larger and more conveniently situated Pravarapura, and embellished it with a group of temples, chaityas, and monasteries, vestiges of which still remain to testify to the magnificence of their founder. But his greatest memorial is the superb temple of Martand,[1] the most striking example of ancient Kashmir architecture that now survives. He distributed even-handed bounty among Brahmans and Buddhists. Among his public works is mentioned the construction of a series of water-wheels for irrigating the arid plateau of Chakradhar below Vijabror.

But Lalitaditya, though a great conqueror and ordinarily a just ruler, had certain defects of character, among which the most noticeable was hard drinking. It is related that in one of his drunken fits he commanded—like Alexander on a similar occasion—the city of

[1] See p. 131.

Srinagar to be set on fire. His minister, however, saved the city, and satisfied his drunken whim at the same time, by setting on fire a large number of distant hayricks. The king was far too tipsy to be able to distinguish between a bonfire of hay and a burning town. But it must be said to his credit that next morning he showed profound contrition for his insensate conduct, and directed his ministers not to carry out any orders that he might issue when drunk. Lalitaditya's last testament is an especially interesting document of Machiavellian wisdom, illustrative as much of the king's policy towards his subjects, as of his views on the administration of the country.

JAYAPIDA-VINAYADITYA.—Lalitaditya's grandson, Jayapida-Vinayaditya, ruled for thirty-one years in the latter part of the eighth century A.D. At first he attempted to follow in the footsteps of his illustrious grandfather, but towards the end of his reign he degenerated into a cruel, overbearing and exacting tyrant, and finally met an untimely end at the hands of the outraged Brahmans who had suffered the most by his rapacity. He founded the town of Jayapura-Andarkot near Sumbal.

Jayapida was followed by a series of weak kings, in whose reigns ministers rose to unprecedented power. For nearly the whole of the first half of the ninth century Utpala and his four brothers, the brothers of a low-born concubine of the lascivious king Lalitapida, held the reins of absolute power in their hands. They usurped all the offices, and gave up the country to plunder and rapine, though at the same time they founded a number of towns and religious edifices, some of which still survive in name. Their career of lawlessness was crowned by an intestine war which culminated in the death of the four younger brothers. Utpala, the eldest and only surviving brother, acquired almost regal power, which was consolidated by his son Sukhavarman, who was king in all but name. Even this pretence was dropped after Sukhavarman's death, when his son Avantivarman was proclaimed king.

AVANTIVARMAN.—Avantivarman (A.D. 855-883) is one of the most lovable persons in the lengthy narrative of the Kashmir historian. The scion of a family of noblemen, who had risen from a particularly low origin to the position of all-powerful king-makers, he possessed all the vigour of a self-made man who had graduated in the hard school of adversity. He was a rare combination of strength and gentleness, and the first and most conscientious servant of the state. But when he ascended the throne his powerful cousins were not disposed to submit to the inevitable as meekly as did the *roi fainéant* whom he had displaced; they had to be thrashed into submission, and that they were. His next care was to give a much-needed rest to the country, which had for nearly a century been distracted by the feuds of powerful barons and the rapacious administration of the Kayasthas, (clerks). Avantivarman's wise rule of twenty-eight years gave the long-suffering people the necessary time to recover from their prolonged nightmare. His triumphs were essentially those of peace, as the triumphs of his great predecessor Lalitaditya were those of war. His pacification of the country, though not described in as great detail as the other episodes of his reign, seems to have been no easy task. In his time first appeared a member of that turbulent class of Damaras, the feudal barons of Kashmir, who during the feeble rule of his successors inflicted untold misery upon the hapless kingdom by their constant and bloody warfare against each other and against the crown. But Avantivarman seems to have kept them in rigid check, as is evidenced by the draconian judgment of his minister Sura upon the powerful baron Dhanva, whom he had killed first and—unlike even the proverbial Jedwood justice—did not even try afterwards. But though the curbing of the restless Damaras was essential to the stability of his own rule and to the peace of his subjects, it is mainly upon his public works, which conferred a lasting boon on the country, and upon his munificent patronage of learning, that his claim to immortality rests.

The chief bane of the valley had for ages been the excess of its water and its liability to floods. A very considerable portion of the land was permanently submerged, and even moderate rainfall resulted in deluging the major part of what remained. The result was a chronic famine. The king, who recognised the necessity of taking prompt and effective action, engaged the services of an eminent Kashmiri engineer, Suyya by name, whose dredging operations at Baramula were so successful that they resulted in an immediate and permanent fall of nearly eighty-four per cent. in the price of paddy. The measures taken by him for confining the rivers and rivulets within their natural boundaries and the regulation of water supply in the arid *karewas* (plateaus), which today are comparatively unproductive, are too numerous to be detailed here.

Among the king's religious foundations is that gem of architecture the Avantisvami temple of Avantipura.[1]

In his efforts to confer upon the country the benefits of peace, the king was ably seconded by his untiring lieutenant, the minister Śura, who had helped him to the throne, and who in spite of the unquestioning obedience he accorded to his sovereign seems to have inspired him with such awe that the latter did not, or could not, reveal his real faith until his dying day. This minister was, like his master, a generous patron of learning, and not only conferred upon the poets, philosophers, and rhetoricians of his day land and fortunes, but, what is very unusual, went so far as to give them seats in the king's council.

ŚANKARAVARMAN (A.D. 883-902) AND HIS SUCCESSORS.—The disintegrating elements in the state, whose progress Avantivarman's strong arm had barely been able to check, broke loose again after his death. Śankaravarman earned lasting infamy by being the author of an ingenious system of exactions by which he reduced the country to misery and impoverishment. But even his cynical oppression was nothing compared with the gross misrule which followed his death. No less than ten sovereigns occupied the throne in the short period of thirty-four years between his death and the third restoration of Chakravarman. Power was entirely in the hands of the Tantrins, who in their close military organisation resembled the Praetorian guards of

[1] See p. 119.

Rome, and who, as might be expected, abused their strength in the same shameless manner. Kings and noblemen vied with each other in buying the favour of this formidable and fickle multitude. No sooner did the crown encircle the brows of one candidate than it was snatched away by another, who had paid a higher bribe and who in his turn was served in similar fashion. No price was deemed too high to purchase the crown; kings squandered their revenues, queens bartered their honour, the son intrigued against his father, and the father set assassins upon his offspring; all lost their sense of truth and dignity for the acquisition, howsoever temporary, of the fatal reward. At last in A.D. 936 the deposed king Chakravarman invoked the aid of the Damaras, the feudal barons of the land, and succeeded with their powerful assistance in annihilating the Tantrins who had so long held the crown as a pawn.

In thus getting rid of the Tantrins by the aid of the barons, the country only passed from one trouble to another. For over two centuries the land lay at the mercy of an hereditary class, whose possessions enabled them to lie secure in their own demesnes, wherefrom they scoured the surrounding country for plunder. The king and the ministers he usually chose for the sole purpose of pandering to his pleasures were far too busy in levying imposts for defraying the cost of their whims, to think of restoring anything like order in the unfortunate country. Government there was none. The king was remarkable only for the extraordinary and, in modern times, unthinkable pitch to which he carried his licence. A curious fatality seems to have followed the Kashmir rulers of this period. Princes who before their accession had given promise of a brave and virtuous career proved, as kings, even more dissolute, pusillanimous, and tyrannical than their predecessors. For two long and weary centuries the court of Kashmir was the Pandora-box of all the evils that afflict humanity, the home of assassins, stranglers, and poisoners. Dissolute ministers of state, pettifogging functionaries as generals of armies, outcastes as reigning queens and kings, whose most innocent recreation was gross buffoonery—such was the administration under which "the Happy Valley" was made unhappy in those centuries. The state of Kashmir in the tenth and eleventh centuries forms a close parallel with that of Italy under Pope Alexander VI and Caesar Borgia. But the Italian popes and their satellites often differed from the Kashmiri kings in that their evil lives were at any rate relieved by the display of commanding talents.

HARSHA.—This misrule culminated in the reign of Harsha (A.D. 1089-1101), whose usually clouded intellect seems to have been, on rare occasions, illuminated by transitory flashes of intelligence, during which he proved himself a liberal patron of learning and music. He appears to have possessed some skill in the composition of popular songs. But his neglect of state affairs was so outrageous that in his reign murders were committed on highways in broad daylight, and even the sanctity of the king's own apartments was not respected by daring robbers. Foodstuffs and other commodities rose to fabulous prices; famine and plague committed such ravages among the people that few were left to cremate or bury the dead, and the river was swollen with floating corpses. To crown all, the king himself ordered the assassination of members of his family and a general massacre of the landed aristocracy—an order which was partly carried out. But even the endurance of a Kashmiri has an end, though it usually takes a long time to awaken him into activity. When Harsha's nephews Uchchala and Sussala raised the standard of rebellion, soldier and priest, prince and peasant, all flocked to it with equal zeal. The palace was given up to flames, the queens burnt to death, the heir-apparent killed, and the king, who was deserted by everybody and had taken refuge in a beggar's hovel, was hunted down and slain without mercy. With him ended the first Lohara dynasty.

UCHCHALA.—Then Uchchala (A.D. 1101-1111), the elder of the two rebel brothers, ascended the throne. His first care was to disarm his troublesome allies, the barons; this he effected more by diplomacy than by force. He kept firm control upon his government, overhauled the bureaucracy, rigorously punished official abuses, administered justice with a rare impartiality and insight into his subjects' character, listened to the grievances of his people, and redressed them as far as lay in his power. He was in the habit of moving about incognito, like the great Caliph Harun-al-Rashid, to discover the causes of distress and unrest among the people; and he sold royal grain at cheap rates for the benefit of the famine-stricken inhabitants of the city. He was energetic in stopping rebellions before they could assume formidable dimensions. But his besetting sin was his haughtiness, which alienated all his dependents and eventually led to his murder.

SUSSALA.—Sussala, who was crowned king in A.D. 1112, wreaked terrible vengeance upon his brother's assassins, and continued to rule peacefully and well until 1120, when he was dispossessed by Bhikshachara, the grandson of Harsha. After a few months, Sussala regained his throne in 1121 and reigned until his murder in 1128. The latter part of his reign was disfigured by acts of oppression and cruelty; but it must be admitted that even in his worst days the administration did not degenerate to the low moral and political standard of his predecessors of the first Lohara dynasty.

JAYASIMHA (A.D. 1128-1155).—His eldest son and successor, Jayasimha, is a very remarkable figure in the history of Kashmir. Though by no means deficient in personal courage, he preferred to gain his ends by the safer and more secret methods of diplomacy and bribery. Where both craft and force had failed he did not shrink from having recourse to assassination. In gaining his ends he was absolutely without scruple in his choice of means. He was courteous to all who approached him, considerate to his servants and subjects, generous to his enemies when they had been deprived of their sting, relentless in the prosecution of his schemes, and possessed of a calm and smiling exterior which concealed a deep underlying purpose. His position on the throne was at first extremely precarious, and if he ultimately emerged triumphant over his numerous enemies and succeeded in giving peace and plenty to the country which he ruled, it was entirely due to his personal abilities, his extraordinary presence of mind, and his resourcefulness in face of misfortune.

The first seventeen years of his reign were occupied in a long and bitter struggle with the barons, who were chafing under the tight control which he attempted to exercise over them. To embarrass him further they set up no less than five pretenders to the throne, some of whom were actually crowned in the outlying district of Lohara. But his opponents were reckoning without their host. One by one both the pretenders and the barons succumbed to the intrigues and coercion which the king, at times so hard pressed as to be almost a prisoner in his own house, incessantly employed against them; till in 1145 he was free from all obstacles to his authority, and the people were saved from the multitude of pests who had made the valley such a hell to them. Kalhana, his contemporary, sums up the account of his rule in the following appreciative verse: " He restored to this land which, owing to the baseness of the time, was like a decayed forest, wealth, population, and habitations." He was an enlightened despot who would have served as a model for Machiavelli's prince.

After the death of Jayasimha[1] the country again reverted to its chronic state of decrepitude. The two centuries that elapsed between the passing away of Jayasimha and the transfer of the throne to the Muslim Shah Mir produced no king possessing genius enough to consolidate his kingdom. If the valley escaped being annexed by the Muslim rulers of India, it was due to its natural isolation and to the physical difficulties its conquest presented, rather than to its military strength and abundant resources. But, at last, in the reign of Suhadeva (A.D. 1300-1 to 1319-20), the clouds began to gather thickly upon the political horizon of Kashmir. Dulucha (Zulqadar Khan), who, according to Abul Fazl, was the chief commander of the armies of the king of Qandahar, penetrated into the valley, and though the king

---

[1] My chief authorities for the period from 1155, the year of Jayasimha's death, to 1587, the year of Akbar's conquest of Kashmir, are the chronicles of Jonaraja, Srivara, and Prajyabhatta and Suka.

bought him off, the invader seems to have made a mental reservation when entering into agreement. For, after he had accepted the money, he commenced to plunder, burn, and slay, with judicial impartiality and scientific precision. When at length the approach of the winter obliged him to leave the country, he left behind him not the flourishing homes of teeming thousands, but smouldering ruins. But the Nemesis of his misdeeds overtook him ere he was well out of the country which he had mercilessly put to fire and the sword; the greater part of his army perished in the snow which surprised them in the passes as they were leaving.

RINCHANA'S INVASION.—All the while that Dulucha was harrying Kashmir, Rinchana, the son of a Tibetan chieftain, was hovering upon the mountains ready to swoop down upon the prostrate country and to gather what was left after Dulucha's invasion. Ramachandra, a patriotic nobleman, offered obstinate resistance to him. When the latter could not overcome him in open fight, he had recourse to treachery, in which he was successful.

RINCHANA KING.—Ramachandra was murdered and his wife (or, as some say, his daughter) Kota was forced to marry the enemy. Rinchana's way to the throne was now clear. Suhadeva was promptly slain, the invader stepped into his place, and ruled for three years (1319-20 to 1322-23) with unexpected munificence and vigour. In the administration of justice he seems to have rigidly adhered to the principles of truth and equity. His desire to be admitted into the fold of the Hindu religion was thwarted by the blind prejudice of the Brahmans, who would have nothing to do with an outcaste Bhotta. Naturally, then, he turned towards the more democratic Islam, and entrusted his infant son by Kota to the care of the Muslim Shah Mir, who had come to Kashmir in A.D. 1313, and had taken service with king Suhadeva. The guardianship of the heir-apparent and the untimely death of Rinchana only three years after his accession were turned by the needy adventurer to his own personal advantage. He did not crown Haidar, his ward; and as he was not yet powerful enough to usurp the kingdom himself, he invited and enthroned Udyanadeva, a scion of the old Hindu dynasty, who, since the invasion of Dulucha, had been living as a refugee in Gandhara.

Curiously enough, the new king not only succeeded Rinchana upon his throne, but also married the widowed queen, who bore him an heir.

But the part that Shah Mir took in the restoration of the old dynasty was not actuated by any gratitude towards the family which had provided him with the means of comfort when he was a homeless wanderer. From the moment of his advent into Kashmir, he seems to have had his eye upon the throne, which he knew by experience was vacant for whoever possessed the longest sword and the strongest arm. All authority was undermined by the dissensions of the nobles. Udyanadeva was too weak to curb their power, and spent his time mostly in the performance of the duties prescribed by his religion. Moreover, he was completely under the control of his domineering wife, Kota.

Shah Mir gradually strengthened his hands by matrimonial alliances with the more powerful families. Many of the nobles who were needy he subsidised, and those that remained he coerced into neutrality. He kept the king and queen in perpetual terror by threatening to raise Haidar, Rinchana's son, to the throne. By the year 1337-38, when Udyanadeva died, the extent of the king's authority was reduced to the precincts of the capital. Shah Mir was the real ruler of the whole country.

Kota Devi.—The queen Kota now ascended the throne herself, but her triumph was short-lived. Her capable minister, Bhatta Bhikshana, was taken off his guard and assassinated by Shah Mir, and Kota, who at that time was in a position to bring the murderer to book, was dissuaded from taking vigorous action by her own counsellors, who doubtless were in Shah Mir's pay. The opportunity thus let slip never recurred, and the queen had afterwards to repent at leisure for what she had neglected to do promptly. Shah Mir now openly meditated treason, and made himself master of the capital, which the queen had left temporarily. He then proceeded to Andarkot and besieged her in the fort there. Kota, being now hopeless and helpless, surrendered on the explicit stipulation that she would share the throne with her conqueror. But her better nature seems to have reasserted itself at the last moment. When she entered the bridal chamber of Shah Mir she stabbed herself with her own dagger in the presence of the husband who had till then been her servant and whose embrace she loathed more than the terrors of the grave.[1]

Thus passed away (1337-38) the last representative of the mediæval Hindu royalty of Kashmir. She died, though she had not been in her lifetime, a worthy daughter of Lalitaditya and of Avantivarman.

SHAH MIR SHAMS-UD-DIN (A.D. 1337).—Shah Mir now ascended the throne under the title of Sultan Shams-ud-din. The most notable act of his reign was the grant of relief in the taxes, which were weighing very heavily upon the country. He " fixed the assessment on land at 17 per cent. of the gross produce."[2] Islam made much progress during the reigns of the first Muslim kings, but the change of masters was not accompanied by any change in the policy of the administration of the state. The same wearisome round of pleasure, the same petty politics, and the same bickerings among the landed noblemen that had characterised the reigns of the later Hindu rulers were continued in the time of their successors, the independent Sultans of Kashmir, who merely carried on the traditions which they had inherited. Sanskrit, corrupted by the admixture of numerous Persian and Arabic technical terms, was still largely used as the official language. The majority of the people were Muslims, but it was Islam of a type that would have astonished the orthodox Arab. The old places of worship still retained their sanctity, the only innovation being that the Hindu image had given place to the tomb of a Muslim saint. Muslim Kashmir

---

[1] According to another tradition she and her two sons were captured by Shah Mir and thrown into prison, in which they languished till their death.

[2] Briggs, *Ferishta*.

teems, to this day, with numberless little shrines and *ziarats* which bear the unmistakable stamp of their Hindu origin. Conversion from one faith to another left the old manners, the customs, and even the superstitions, of the people intact. As a rule the kings were far too busy with their own troubles and pleasures to bestow much thought upon their subjects, who doubtless were content to plod their own way unmolested, happy if forgotten.

SHAHAB-UD-DIN (A.D. 1355-1374).—After Shah Mir, or, as he styled himself, Shams-ud-din, the first king of mark in his dynasty was Shahab-ud-din (A.D. 1355-1374). In the early part of his reign he made a brilliant raid on north-western India and overran the territories adjoining the upper courses of the Indus (Ohind, etc.), sacked Peshawar and seriously threatened Ghazni and Kandahar. The snowy barrier of the Hindu Kush seems to have forced him to retrace his steps to the plains. He marched eastwards as far as the Sutlej, where he met and exchanged greetings with the Raja of Nagarkot, who was returning from a similar expedition from Delhi. The year 1361, the sixth of his reign, was marked by a disastrous flood over nearly the whole valley, which forced the inhabitants to take refuge in the uplands and hills. His indignation at the suggestion of Udayasri, his minister, to melt the brass image of the Brihat Buddha and coin the metal into money, is eloquent of the tolerant character of these early Muslim rulers of Kashmir. The latter part of his reign was not a happy one for himself, chiefly because of the baneful influence which Lasa, the young niece of his queen Lakshmi, whom he had taken as a concubine, exercised upon his mind. She induced him to exile his three grown-up sons; and though he recalled Hasan, his eldest born, when he felt his end drawing near, he was not destined to see him again. In the absence of the legitimate heir, Qutb-ud-din, the late king's brother, ascended the throne. In the annals of Muslim rulers of most countries the maxim " first come, first served " finds frequent illustration. According to Firishta, " This prince was remarkable for his attention to public business, which he transacted in person and gener-

ally with justice and moderation." In his old age two sons were born
to him, the elder of whom, Sikandar, succeeded him while yet a minor,
in A.D. 1390.

SIKANDAR BUT-SHIKAN (A.D. 1390-1414).—On Sikandar's accession to the throne Islam adopted a more defined and aggressive attitude.
His predecessors had not been troubled with any scruples of conscience
when expediency had urged upon them the necessity of stretching a
point in favour of their Hindu subjects. Qutb-ud-din performed a
Hindu religious sacrifice and bestowed grants of land upon Brahmans
and other religious corporations, to avert an impending famine. The
birth of his son, Sikandar, was attributed to the efficacy of the magic
pill of a Hindu ascetic. Sikandar himself was married to a Hindu
lady, Sri Sobha, and during the earlier part of his reign was content
to follow in the footsteps of his tolerant predecessors. But his liberal
patronage of literature attracted a host of foreign scholars, who, being
uncompromising zealots, were naturally shocked at the amicable relations that existed between the Muslims and the "infidels." That
the influx of these foreign literati was not viewed without misgiving
by the Kashmiris may be perceived from the description of the
incident by Jonaraja in the following terms: "As the fledgling pigeon
is surrounded on all sides by crows, so was the king surrounded by
Yavanas, who became his preceptors, his retainers, his servants, his
favourites, and even his relatives." Among the foreigners was Mir
Sayyid Muhammad Hamadani, son of Mir Sayyid Ali Hamadani
(Shah Hamadan), who is said to have obtained complete mastery over
the young king's mind and exercised it for the purpose of purging
Kashmir of all heterodoxy.

But in spite of all the pressure that the Maulvis brought to bear
upon him, the king persisted in his endeavour to keep his hands clean
of religious persecution. Fate, however, had ordained otherwise;
and the king at last reluctantly yielded to the specious arguments
of his minister Suhabhatta, who had originally been a Hindu,
but since his conversation to Islam hated his former co-religionists

with the deep-rooted and implacable hatred of the neophyte.   All traces of the king's reluctance, whether real or simulated, vanished when he had once given his consent.   In Sikandar religion ran amok. Many bent before the storm, but those who did not were ruthlessly broken.   Cremation of the dead was interdicted, wearing of caste marks was prohibited, and orders were issued proscribing residence of any but Muslims in the country.   When the people began to leave in large numbers, the king and his minister permitted them to proceed to the frontier and then closed all passages of exit.   There they were caught in a trap, driven back, and given the alternative of death or conversion.   The majority succumbed and abjured their faith, a few brave souls gave up their lives as willing martyrs to their cause.   The great shrines of Chakradhara and Vijayeśa were razed to the ground; the Martand and Avantipur temples were so irreparably ruined that even the manner of their destruction is, to this day, a matter of con-jecture.   Jonaraja, whose feelings would naturally be more embittered against Suhabhatta than against Sikandar, tells us that " there was no city or town, no village or forest, where an abode of the gods escaped destruction by Suhabhatta.   All the images of the gods were broken (with no more consideration than if) they had been mere stones, but no misfortune was seen (to befall) the perpetrators (of the deed) as (had always been the case) of yore."

The year A.D. 1398 is memorable in the annals of Hindustan for the invasion by Timur and his Tartar hordes.   The empire of the Tughlaks had for many years been tottering to its fall.   On the ele-vation, in 1394, of the minor Mahmud to the throne of Delhi, Gujarat, Khandesh, Malava, and Jaunpur threw off the feeble yoke of the Sultan of Delhi, and asserted complete independence.   While the different chieftains were parcelling out the empire between themselves, the Tartar hurricane burst over their heads and involved them all, princes and peasants, oppressors and oppressed, in one common ruin. Kashmir was not an indifferent spectator while this tragedy was being enacted.   Timur rewarded Sikandar for his neutrality with the gift of a couple of elephants, whose uncouth shape and extraordinary bulk seem to have considerably stirred the imagination of the simple Kashmiris. On Timur's return from Delhi, Sikandar marched out to meet him, but hearing that he was expected to make a present of " three thousand horses and one hundred thousand pieces of gold as an offering," [1] he quietly retraced his steps and contented himself with sending excuses.

Another expedition more creditable to his arms was Sikandar's invasion of North-West India, in which he subdued the city of Ohind and married the daughter of its chief, Firoz. This lady was the mother of Sikandar's illustrious son Zain-ul-abidin. Both these events took place long before Sikandar had earned or deserved the title of *But-shikan*. The assistance he rendered to the Gakkhar freebooter Jasrat Khan (who had been captured by Timur and taken by him to Samarqand, and who had, on his captor's demise, made his escape to India) in obtaining possession of certain tracts of the country in the north of the Panjab, and the marriage of his own two daughters to the rulers of Sind and Ohind, belong to the later part of his reign.

The reign of terror which Sikandar had inaugurated in Kashmir continued with unabated vigour even after his death in 1414, through the efforts of his minister Suhabhatta, who wielded great power as long as he lived. He died of consumption some years after the death of Sikandar.

ZAIN-UL-ABIDIN (A.D. 1421-1472). — Zain-ul-abidin succeeded to the throne of his feeble brother Ali Shah in the year 1421 at the early age of seventeen; but his youth by no means stood in the way of his vigorously putting a stop to the abuses prevalent in the country. His mission in life was to redress the wrongs and heal the wounds which his father and brother had inflicted upon the unhappy Hindus of the valley. In this he was entirely successful. As his activities extended to the overhauling and readjustment of the whole administrative machinery, his character will be better understood if we

---

[1] Briggs, *Ferishta*.

briefly mention his reforms under detailed heads, the place of honour being, without question, reserved for his proclamation of peace and goodwill to all mankind.

An idea of the barbarism to which Kashmir had been reduced at that period will be gained by the fact that when Zain-ul-abidin was suffering from a severe eruption, no physician could be found willing or able to attend him.   At last one Siryabhatta was induced, after promise of personal safety, to treat the king!   Refusing to accept any reward for the successful treatment, except the boon of mercy for his co-religionists, he was made Chief Justice and High Treasurer, with injunctions to ameliorate the condition of the Hindus.   This he did very naturally with enthusiasm.   The destruction of Hindu scriptures was forthwith stopped.   The Brahmans who had fled were repatriated, their lands and property which had been usurped by Muslims were restored to them.   The annual capitation tax of two *palas* of silver, which weighed heavily upon them, was reduced to a nominal fee of a single *māsha* and later was entirely abolished.   Sacrifices and pilgrimages were again permitted.   Prohibition against cremation was removed.   The schools were reopened, and Hindu boys were allowed to study their own scriptures.   The king carried his predilection for Hindu religion much farther than toleration.   He himself attended Hindu shrines, performed sacrifices, built monasteries, and not only acquired a thorough knowledge of Sanskrit, but employed all his available time in the study of its sacred books.   In his last years, which were made unhappy through his own infirmity and the feuds between his sons, he found his sole consolation in the study of the transcendental philosophy of the *Yogavāsishṭha*.

In the administration of justice he showed a remarkable combination of mercy, sternness, and shrewd common sense.   He thoroughly purged the law courts of corruption and bribery, and anticipated the prison reforms of the nineteenth century by instituting a system of prison industries, pottery being one of them.   Thieves and other criminals, who formerly would have suffered instant execution, were

now made to work as labourers on public works, this being probably
the chief reason why his reign was so prolific of works of public utility
which have lasted down to recent times. The assessment of land was
fixed at a reasonable rate, and in the newly irrigated area of Zainagir
near Sopor the proportion was kept as low as one-seventh of the gross
produce. The prices of imports, which then were arbitrarily fixed by
the vendors thereof, were now regulated, consideration in each case
being paid to the carriage and other charges. The prices of commodities were also regulated by monthly notifications. This was a great
boon in Kashmir, where, owing to the want of communications, profit-
eering has many attractions and chances of immediate success. The
system was instituted of having the deeds of sale of property sealed
with the king's seal, absence of this having been the cause of much
forgery. In the distracted times of his two immediate predecessors
the criminal classes had gathered much strength. Even during the
long reign of Zain-ul-abidin, thefts seem to have been by no means
rare, and the means of tracing them were few. The king hit upon a
plan which seems to have met with appreciable success, though in
some cases the innocent must have suffered with the guilty. This
was, to make the villages and the forest communities, among whom the
traveller sojourned for the period during which he was robbed, responsible for the loss. For the convenience of travellers rest-houses
were built in many places on the principal roads. As the chronicler
says, " the king administered punishment and reward to his subjects
with due regard (to their merits), and watched over them with care as
the husbandman watches over his crop, supplying water or keeping
the field dry as may seem suitable."

His patronage of merit, irrespective of caste or creed, is illustrated
by the choice he made of his important officials, among whom were the
Buddhist Tilakacharya, Prime Minister, the Brahman Siryabhatta,
Chief Justice, and the Muslim Darya Khan, who eventually succeeded
Tilaka in the premiership. The king's own literary predilections
and the encouragement given to men of learning by his minister

Siryabhatta induced a large number of scholars to flock to the Kashmir court. This was the period when the Kashmiri-Persian literature, which until the last quarter of a century occupied an almost exclusive place in the education and culture of the official, or *karkun*, class of Kashmiri pandits, began to grow. The king was personally interested in the movement, and caused a number of the more important Sanskrit works to be translated into Persian. The growth of the indigenous Kashmiri literature was given a strong impetus. Utta-Soma and Yuddhabhatta wrote biographies of the king in the vernacular, and Bhattavatara, who is said to have studied the *Shāhnāma*, wrote the *Jainavilāsa*. The king himself composed two works in Persian, the first being a treatise in the form of questions and answers on the manufacture of fireworks, and the second, entitled *Shikayat* (the Plaint), a poem written in his old age when he was completely disillusioned by his misfortunes, and the death of his ministers and companions had left him lonely and world-weary, and when he saw his life-work undone by the mutual animosity of his worthless sons. This poem may have been a sort of " The Vanity of Human Wishes."

But his favourite literary pursuit was undoubtedly the study of Sanskrit, to which, as has been said, he devoted a considerable part of his time. Without counting the historians Jonaraja and Śrivara, the most notable scholars who attended his court were Karpurabhatta, the physician; Ruppabhatta, the astronomer; Ramananda, who wrote an exposition of the *Mahābhāshya*; and Yuddhabhatta, who, having during Suhabhatta's régime gone to Maharashtra, and studied there the *Atharvaveda*, which until then seems to have been not commonly known in Kashmir, returned at the invitation of Siryabhatta and pro-mulgated the study of that Veda in his native land. A copy of the *Atharvaveda* was also presented to the king himself, who, further to increase its popularity, established schools in which the scholars were fed, lodged and taught, at the expense of the state.

Altogether, Zain-ul-abidin's reign was the Augustan era of later Kashmiri-Sanskrit literature.

The maintenance of a magnificent court and a galaxy of brilliant scholars must have meant much expense, which the revenue of the depopulated valley was ill able to provide. Zain-ul-abidin therefore started the working of copper mines, the collection of gold dust in the Ladakh rivers, and the construction of an extensive system of canals which irrigated large tracts of heretofore arid land and yielded considerable revenue, by which he acquired wealth without imposing additional taxes upon the already over-taxed people.

A prominent feature in the landscape of the Kashmir valley are the large waterless alluvial plateaus, locally called *wudars*, which occupy a considerable part of its area. Unlike the lower parts of the valley, which are irrigated by the numerous rivers and rivulets with which the country abounds, the productivity of these *wudars* is wholly dependent upon the uncertain rainfall. The crops they usually yield are, therefore, naturally fitful and meagre, the harvest often being nil. Zain-ul-abidin's keen eye was struck with the immense possibilities of these plateaus if they could be permanently irrigated. Fortunately, Kashmir, surrounded as it is on all sides by high mountains, capped with everlasting snows, in whose ravines are huge glaciers which feed innumerable perennial streams, offers peculiar facilities for artificial irrigation, as was demonstrated by the large network of canals which nearly doubled the arable land of the valley in the time of Zain-ul-abidin. Most of the canals fell into disuse in the aforementioned troublous times, but one or two have been renovated during the last three decades. Chief among these canals were (1) one which irrigated the lands round Kakapur; (2) the Tsakadar canal brought from Nandamarg; (3) the Karala canal, which irrigated the plateau between Shupayan and Romuh, where a colony of Brahmans was settled; (4) the canal to Avantipur, which is extant to this day, but runs only as far as Midur and Rajpur; (5) the Shah Kul, which branches off from the Sindh near Wusan and runs through the *pargana* of Lar, to Manasbal; the town of Saphala, modern Safapor, was built near its termination; (6) another canal, branching from the Sindh, ran to the capital, where it supplied water to the Jama' Masjid, and emptied itself in the Mar canal. This used to run through the city as recently as twenty years ago and was known as the Lachma Kul; (7) the canal from the river Pohur to irrigate the highlands of Sopor; and (8) the most important of all, the Shah Kul of Martand, the recent renovation of which has converted the arid plains which stretch for miles on three sides of the temple into a smiling garden of waving corn.

His public works were not limited to the excavation of canals. He was an enlightened promoter of the architecture and the arts of the country. His name is to this day associated with the erection of the bridge Zaina Kadal, still the most important commercial thoroughfare of Srinagar, the construction of the town of Zainagir, and of the island of Zainalank in the Wular lake. But by far the greater part of his secular and religious foundations have perished.

He gave a strong impetus to the manufacture of paper, shawls, and embroidered tapestry, for which Kashmir has always been famous. He promoted the silk industry by inviting weavers from Khurasan and settling them in the country. It was in his reign, in the year A.D. 1466, that firearms were first introduced into Kashmir.

His relations with foreign powers were not restricted to the petty principalities bordering upon Kashmir. He himself conquered Sindh and a portion of Tibet, occupying the latter territory permanently. According to Abul Fazl, Sultan Abu Said Mirza sent him presents of Arab horses and dromedaries from Khurasan, and Bahlol Lodi, king of Delhi, as well as Sultan Mahmud of Gujarat, were in friendly relations with him. The contemporary chronicler reports that he exchanged presents with the kings of Misr (Egypt) and Mecca; and that he exercised control over the rulers of Gandhara, Jammu, and Rajauri and the Gakkhar tribes of northern Panjab. It is certain that he assisted Jasrat Khan Gakkhar in consolidating his authority over a considerable part of the Panjab.

To estimate the abstemiousness of Zain-ul-abidin's character and the extent to which the transcendental philosophy of Vasishtha had influenced his mind, it is only necessary to record that he, a Muslim ruler, married a single wife and remained faithful to her throughout his life. This may not sound, to modern ears, an extraordinary achievement, but those who know the numerical strength of the harems of Oriental potentates of that time will appreciate the fact.

Zain-ul-abidin's last years were embittered by the mutual jealousies of his factious and dissipated sons, which, on more than one occasion, broke out into actual warfare, and necessitated the exile of one or the other of them. The king was, moreover, in the grievous position of having outlived his age. He had outlived his wife, his friends, his colleagues, and his usefulness. He felt his authority slipping away from his hands, his sons were openly rebellious, his personal attendants were daily deserting him, everybody was waiting for him to make his exit from the stage which he had filled so long. The mighty monarch, the benefactor of humanity, the patron of arts and sciences, was forgotten. He refused to see anyone, shut himself up in a room, spent his last days in hearing from Srivara the *moksho-paya*, "the way to salvation," that panacea of the Hindus for all their physical ills and mental worries. At last, after a long and eventful reign of more than half a century, a merciful Providence relieved him of the life which had grown a burden to him. While yet a beardless boy, he had fought his way to the throne; before he had reached the prime of his life, he had seen nearly all his aspirations crowned with unprecedented success, and ere he felt old age coming over him, he had drained to its dregs the cup of disappointment. There are few more pathetic figures in the annals of India than this solitary old man refusing to be consoled for a life of earnest endeavour, splendid achievement, and irremediable failure. No wonder that he wrote a *Shikayat*, accusing Destiny of flirting with him with a false show of happiness which he had, Tantalus-like, been ever pursuing and never quite overtaking; still less wonder that he flew for refuge to a philosophy which taught that life is vanity and the world an illusion.

So died Zain-ul-abidin, commonly called Badshah, "the great king," of Kashmir.[1]

HAIDAR SHAH.—After his death, in 1472, the dynasty of Shah Mir did not produce any sovereign of outstanding ability. Haidar, the son and successor of Badshah, whose behaviour had hastened the declining king's end, started afresh the persecutions which his father had taken such pains to abolish. His administration of justice was capricious and arbitrary to the extent of making children suffer for the sins of their fathers.

He was succeeded by his son Hasan, who opened his régime by the re-establishment of the laws of his grandfather and the release of all political prisoners. He also imitated his grandfather in the erection of numerous public buildings, and is said to have issued a new and peculiar kind of coinage. But he was dominated by his Sayyid wife, who used her power to forward the interests of her numerous kinsfolk, who rose to such predominance that Malik Ahmad, the chief minister, was forced to expel them from Kashmir. They were, however, soon recalled, and after bringing about the disgrace and imprisonment of the minister assumed absolute power. The king's death occurred shortly after this, not without a suspicion of foul play on the part of the Sayyids.

The accounts we have of the century between the first enthrone-ment of Muhammad Shah, the infant son of Hasan, and the annexation of Kashmir to the Mughal empire, are of little interest. No less than twenty sovereigns, including the usurper Mirza Haidar of Kashgar, ruled during this period. Of these, Muhammad ruled four times, Nazuk Shah thrice, and Fath Shah twice. Before the dethroned prince was out of the country he was recalled and reinstated. There was no rule and there was no ruler except in name. Every person was a man-at-arms, ready to hire himself to whoever had the longest purse. The only real national movement was the resistance offered

---

[1] The relatively long account of Zain-ul-abidin's reign is based on the detailed in-formation supplied by Jonaraja and Srivara, who were his contemporaries and historians.

to the Sayyids in the first year of Muhammad Shah's first reign. These foreigners had woefully wronged the Kashmiris, who considered their presence in the country as an affront. All united in the common cause. The Raja of Jammu lent them aid, and the Sayyids, though they had invoked the aid of Tatar Khan, the Lodi governor of the Panjab, were mercilessly slaughtered. But no sooner was the motive for united action removed, than the Kashmiri noblemen fell out among themselves as regards the distribution of the prizes of victory.

The names of Magre and Tsak loom large over a crowd of tribes and clans who exercised arms as a profession and who contended for the possession of supreme power. The Magres were native, while the Tsaks were foreigners, probably of Dard origin, who had become naturalised in Kashmir. Gradually all parties in the country were merged into these two factions, and there ensued a civil war which ended only with the Mughal occupation of the country, though the Magres were playing a distinctly losing game from A.D. 1560, when Ghazi Tsak ousted Habib Shah and occupied the throne himself.

The first reign of Fateh Shah is notable for introduction into Kashmir of the Nurbakhshi sect of Islam by one Shams-ud-din of Iraq. They were vigorously put down by Mirza Haidar. This celebrated Mughal condottiere conquered Kashmir twice, and ruled it from 1541 to 1551. His first invasion was from the side of Ladakh, to which country he had accompanied Sikandar Khan of Kashgar on a crusade against the infidels in A.D. 1533. Though he penetrated into Kashmir and occupied the city for a time, during which his soldiers behaved with ruthless barbarity, he was eventually compelled to come to terms and to make his retreat towards Tibet. His second invasion was effected at the time when Sher Shah was chasing Humayun out of Hindustan. This time he conquered Kashmir on behalf of Humayun, and struck coins in his name. Among other things he occupied his time in writing his valuable *Tārīkh-i-Rashīdī*, which is a history of the Mughals of Central Asia, and also gives an account, unfortunately meagre, of the Kashmir of his day.

Of the dynasty of Tsaks little need be said here. The ferocity of Ghazi Shah, the first ruler of this dynasty, was almost incredible.

Yusuf Shah, the last independent sovereign of Kashmir, or perhaps more correctly the last but one, was anxious to make his submission to Akbar, but his ministers stood in the way and openly defied the emperor's envoy. The first Mughal invasion under raja Bhagavan Das resulted only in a treaty by which the Kashmir king bound himself to pay tribute to the emperor. But Akbar, who had set his heart upon the full and unqualified conquest of the valley, refused to ratify the terms. A second army was set on foot. Yusuf was taken prisoner and endowed with a small *jāgīr* in the distant province of Bihar. His son Yaqub fought hard and persistently for the throne of his father, but was at last compelled to yield, and made to join Yusuf Shah in his inglorious retreat.

The advent of the Mughals in 1587 ushered in the modern age of Kashmir. The conditions of the new rule were entirely different from those which had obtained at any time in the mediæval age. The country now formed part of a mighty empire, and became for more than a century the pleasure garden of the most magnificent court that India has ever seen. The Subadars having learnt the art of government at the seat of an empire which was made up of a vast congeries of nations and countries, possessing diverse languages, manners, customs, and religions, naturally displayed far greater breadth of vision and statesmanship in the conduct of their administration than was the case with the indigenous rulers and their ministers, whose limited power and narrowness of jurisdiction only served to increase their rancorous animosity against one another. The realignment and construction, by Muhammad Qasim Khan, Akbar's engineer-in-chief, of the great Imperial route via Gujrat, Bhimber, and Shupayan, which ensured regular communication and safety of traffic and transit with the mainland of India, marks a revolution, scarcely less far-reaching in its results than the opening of the Jhelum Valley Road in our own day. Kashmir was brought into touch with the currents permeating the policy and administration of an extensive empire, and in the presence of mightier issues forgot its own petty squabbles. Its people, the most impulsive in the whole of India, basked in the sunshine of the benign rule of Akbar, whom they almost deified, and with the characteristic inconsistency of a mob, sang hallelujahs over the extinction of a cruel tyranny, to the existence of which they themselves had contributed. The emperors bestowed paternal care upon the valley and its inhabitants. It must, of course, not be understood that this period of a century and more was for Kashmir a long round of unadulterated pleasure. There were governors who in their eagerness to amass fortunes were not always scrupulous in the employment of righteous means only to achieve their object, but they were not many, for the emperor's punishment of such delinquents was sharp and severe. But it is a fact that that century was, on the whole, one of the happiest periods in the history of the country.

Among the writers to whom we owe our knowledge of this period, the most important and exalted are Abul Fazl, the guide, philosopher, friend, and chronicler of Akbar, and the emperor Jahangir himself. The former says that " the country is enchanting, and might fittingly be called a garden of perpetual spring, surrounding a citadel terraced to the skies, and deservedly appropriate to be either the delight of the worldling or the retired abode of the recluse. Its streams are sweet to the taste, its waterfalls music to the ear, and its climate is invigorating. . . . The lands are artificially watered, or dependent on rain for irrigation. The flowers are enchanting. . . . Its spring and autumn are extremely beautiful. The houses are all of wood, and are of four stories and some of more, but it is not the custom to enclose them. Cattle and sundry stores are kept in the lower story, the second contains the family apartments, and in the third and fourth are the household chattels. On account of the abundance of wood and the constant earthquakes, houses of stone and brick are not built, but the ancient temples inspire astonishment. At the present day many of them are in ruins. Woollen fabrics are made in high perfection, especially shawls, which are sent as valuable gifts to many climes. But the bane of this country is its people. Yet, strange to say, notwithstanding its numerous population and the scantiness of the means of subsistence, thieving and begging are rare. Besides plums and mulberries, the fruits are numerous. Melons, apples, peaches, apricots, are excellent. Although the grapes are in plenty, the finer qualities are rare, and the vines bear on mulberry trees. The mulberry is little eaten, its leaves being reserved for the silkworm. The eggs are brought from Gilgit and Little Tibet. . . . The food of the people is chiefly rice, wine, flesh, and various vegetables, and the last mentioned they dry and preserve. Rice is cooked and kept overnight to be eaten. . . . Apparel is generally of wool. . . . There are artificers of various kinds who might be deservedly employed in the greatest cities. The bazar system is little in use, as a brisk traffic is carried on at their own places of business. The people take their pleasure in skiffs upon the lakes, and their hawks strike the wildfowl in mid-air, and bring them to the boats, and sometimes they hold them down in the water in their talons, and stand upon them, presenting an exciting spectacle.

" . . . The carriage of goods is effected by boat, but men also carry great loads over the most difficult country. Boatmen and carpenters drive a thriving trade. The Brahman class is very numerous.

" Although Kashmir has a dialect of its own, their learned books are in the Sanskrit language. They have a separate character which they use for manuscript work, and they write chiefly on *tuz*, which is the bark of a tree. . . . The majority of the narrow-minded conservatives of blind tradition are Sunnis, and there are some Imamis and Nurbakshis, who are perpetually at strife with each other. They are chiefly from Persia and Turkestan. . . . The most respectable class in this country is that of the Brahmans, who, notwithstanding their need of freedom from the bonds of tradition and custom, are true worshippers of God.

" They do not loosen the tongue of calumny against those not of their faith, nor beg, nor importune. They employ themselves in planting fruit trees, and are generally a source of benefit to the people.

"Srinagar is the capital and is 4 *farsakhs* in length. The rivers Bihat, Mar, and Lachmankul flow through it. This has been a flourishing city from ancient times and the home of artificers of various kinds. Beautiful shawls are woven, and they manufacture woollen stuffs extremely soft. Durmah, pattu, and other woollen materials are prepared, but the best are brought from Tibet. . . .

" In the village of Pampur, one of the dependencies of Vihi, there are fields of saffron to the extent of ten or twelve thousand *bighas*, a sight that would enchant the most fastidious (Plate III).

" Adjoining (the city) is a large lake called Dal . . . on its surface a number of floating islands are constructed which are cultivated, and fraudulent people will at times cut off a piece and carry it away to a different position. . . .

" Saffron is also cultivated in Paraspur.

" The system of revenue collection is by appraisement and division of crops, assessments for crops having special rates and cash transactions not being the custom of the country. Some part of the *sā'irjāt* (miscellaneous taxes other than land revenue) cesses, however, are taken in cash. Payment in coin and kind was estimated in *kharwārs* of *shāli* (rice). Although one-third had been for a long time past the nominal share of the state, more than two shares was actually taken. Through His Majesty's justice, it has been reduced to one-half. . . . The revenue, therefore, amounted to 7 krores 46 lakhs 70,411 dams (Rs. 1,866,766-4-5). . . ."[1]

Akbar visited Kashmir thrice, and was so enamoured of it that he designated it his "private garden." His abolition of the capitation tax on the Hindus, the restoration of their lands, and the institution of a permanent land settlement, are still remembered with gratitude by the people of the valley. His most notable monument in the country is

---

[1] *Ain-i-Akbari*, translated by Jarett, vol. ii, pp. 347-371.

the magnificent rampart of the Hari Parbat fort, or, as it was then called, the fort of Nagar Nagar, which he made the military cantonment of Srinagar (Plate XI).   But it was in the time of Jahangir and Shah Jahan that Kashmir became the real pleasure garden of the empire. Jahangir himself states that he considered it bad taste to stretch a carpet on the green sward of the valley.

The best account we have of the visit of a Mughal emperor, and of the condition of Kashmir in the later part of the seventeenth century, is from the pen of François Bernier, the celebrated French physician-traveller, who accompanied Aurangzeb to Kashmir in 1664.   A summary of his account is given below:

"That scarcity of provisions may not be produced in the small kingdom of Kachemire, the king will be followed by a very limited number of individuals.   Of females he takes only ladies of the first rank, the intimate friends of Rauchenara Begam, and those women whose services cannot be dispensed with.   The omrahs and military will also be as few as possible. . . .   The king has a few of the choicest elephants for his baggage and the women of the seraglio . . . also a few mules. . . .   Porters supply the place of camels . . . the king alone has no fewer than six thousand . . . and it is calculated that there are at least fifteen thousand porters already collected at Bhimber; some sent by the governor of Kachemire and by the neighbouring rajas, and others who are come voluntarily in the expectation of earning a little money.   A royal ordinance fixes their pay at ten crowns (Rs. 20) for every hundred pounds weight.   It is computed that thirty thousand will be employed; an enormous number when it is considered that the king and omrahs have been sending forward baggage, and the tradespeople articles of every sort, for the last month.

"The whole kingdom bears the appearance of a fertile and highly cultivated garden.   Villages and hamlets are frequently seen through the luxuriant foliage.   Meadows and vineyards, fields of rice, wheat, hemp, saffron, and many sorts of vegetables, among which are intermingled trenches filled with water, rivulets, canals, and several small lakes, vary the enchanting scene. The whole ground is enamelled with our European flowers and plants, and covered with our apple, pear, plum, apricot, and walnut trees, all bearing fruit in great abundance. The private gardens are full of melons, pateques or watermelons, water parsnips, red beet, radishes, most of pot-herbs and others with which we are unacquainted.

" The capital of Kachemire bears the same name as the kingdom. It is without walls and is not less than three-quarters of a league in length and half a league in breadth. . . . In the town there are two wooden bridges thrown over the river; and the houses, although for the most part of wood, are well built and consist of two or three stories. . . . Most of the houses along the banks of the river have little gardens, which produce a very pretty effect, especially in the spring and summer, when many parties of pleasure take place upon the water. Indeed most houses in the city have also their gardens; and many have a canal, on which the owner keeps a pleasure boat, thus communicating with the lake.

" In truth the kingdom surpasses in beauty all that my warm imagination had anticipated. . . . Jehan-guyre became so enamoured of this little kingdom as to make it the place of his favourite abode, and he often declared that he would rather be deprived of every other province of his mighty empire than lose Kachemire.

" I was quite prepared to witness the emulous contest between the Kachemiry and the Mughal poets. We were no sooner arrived than Aurang-Zebe received from the bards of both nations poems in praise of this favoured land which he accepted and rewarded with kindness. . . .

" The Kachmiris are celebrated for wit, and considered much more intelligent and ingenious than the Indians. In poetry and science they are not inferior to Persians. They are also very active and industrious. The workmanship and beauty of their palekys, bedsteads, trunks, inkstands, boxes, spoons, and various other things, are quite remarkable, and articles of their manufacture are in use in

every part of the Indies. They perfectly understand the art of var-
nishing, and are eminently skilful in closely imitating the beautiful
veins of a certain wood by inlaying with gold threads so delicately
wrought that I never saw anything more elegant or perfect. But what
may be considered peculiar to Kachemire and the staple commodity,
that which particularly promotes the trade of the country, and fills it
with wealth, is the prodigious quantity of shawls which they manufacture, and which gives occupation even to little children. . . .

" The people of Kachemire are proverbial for their complexions
and fine forms. They are well made as the Europeans, and their
faces have neither the Tartar flat nose nor the small pig-eyes that
distinguish the natives of Kacheguer, and which generally mark those
of Great Tibet. The women especially are very handsome; and it
is from this country that nearly every individual, when first admitted
to the court of the Great Mughal, selects wives or concubines, that
his children may be whiter than the Indians, and pass for genuine
Mughals. . . ."[1]

The decline in the fortunes of the Mughal Empire was accompanied by decline in the prosperity of the valley. The *rois fainéants*
who succeeded Aurangzeb lost all hold of their distant possessions.
In 1739, Kashmir was annexed to the kingdom of Kabul by Nadir Shah,
and it remained subject to the dominion of the Afghans until Ranjit
Singh wrested it from the Amir Dost Muhammad in 1819. In 1846,
on the defeat of the Sikhs, it was transferred to Maharaja Gulab Singh
by the British Government. Since then it has been under Dogra
rule.

SALIENT DATES IN KASHMIR CHRONOLOGY

1. Aśoka ... ... 272-232 B.C.
2. Kanishka ... ... circa A.D. 125.
3. Mihirakula ... ... First half of the fifth century A.D.
4. Pravarasena II ... ... End of sixth century A.D.
5. Muktapida-Lalitaditya ... Middle of eighth century A.D.

[1] *Bernier*, p. 390 *f.*

6. Avantivarman	A.D. 856/7 to 883.
7. Śankaravarman	A.D. 883 to 902.
8. Queen Didda	A.D. 980/1 to 1003.
9. Uchchala	A.D. 1101 to 1111.
10. Sussala	A.D. 1112 to 1128.
11. Jayasimha	A.D. 1128 to 1155.
12. Rinchana	A.D. 1319/20 to 1322/23.
13. Shah Mir alias Shams-ud-din	A.D. 1338 to 1341
14. Shihab-ud-din	A.D. 1355/6 to 1374.
15. Sikandar	A.D. 1390 to 1414.
16. Zain-ul-abidin	A.D. 1421-1472.
17. Mirza Haidar Doghlat ...	A.D. 1541-1551.
18. Ghazi Shah Tsak	A.D. 1555.
19. Akbar	A.D. 1556-1605.
20. Jahangir	A.D. 1605-1627.
21. Shah Jahan	A.D. 1627-1658.
22. Nadir Shah	Annexes Kashmir in A.D. 1739.
23. Ahmad Shah Abdali ...	Succeeds Nadir in 1747.
24. Ranjit Singh	Conquers Kashmir in 1819.
25. Gulab Singh...	Acquires the valley of Kashmir from the British in 1846, on payment of one million pounds.

ARCHITECTURAL STYLES[1]

EARLY BUILDINGS (CIRCA A.D. 200 TO 600)

No structural monuments which can, with certainty, be said to belong to the pre-Christian era have yet been discovered in Kashmir. Even the first six centuries A.D. are very meagrely represented; the only monuments which can with certainty be assigned to the Kushan period being the Buddhist structures at Harwan (see pp. 105-111) and Ushkar.

The abundance in which the coins of Indo-Greek, Parthian, and Śaka kings of north-western India were found until recently in Kashmir points to the existence of considerable commercial intercourse, if not actual political connection, between the valley and the principalities of Peshawar and Kabul in the last two centuries B.C. and the first century A.D. It is also certain that in the second century A.D. Kashmir formed part of Kanishka's empire and that, for at least some generations after the death of that emperor, the country remained attached to the kingdom of Gandhara. This long connection with the north-west of India has left an indelible mark upon the character of the Buddhist and Hindu architecture of the valley. The early Buddhist religious edifices of Kashmir have practically the same plan, and probably had the same elevation, as the contemporary Buddhist buildings of Gandhara. There was, however, a considerable difference in the materials used and in the modes of decoration. At Ushkar, for instance, the abundance of local quarries ensured a plentiful supply of stone chips, which the builders turned to excellent advantage. At Harwan, on the other hand, the most easily available building materials

---

[1] This chapter was first published in article form in the *Rupam* of Calcutta.

are the round boulders and pebbles brought down by the Dachigam Nala. Here accordingly we find the chip-masonry of Ushkar replaced by walls built of small pebbles (Plate XVII). The endeavour in each case seems to have been to employ building materials which were as small in size as possible. Probably it was thought that the merit accruing to the donor of a religious structure was commensurate with the amount of labour and care bestowed upon it. But this method carried to excess was bound to lead to disaster. The masons of Harwan, at any rate, seem to have realised early that a pebble wall built in mud, each pebble being not more than one or two inches in diameter, even though it was covered by a coat of plaster, was not a durable structure. In fact, to keep it standing for even a short period was not easy without vigilant care and constant repairs, for every shower of rain was certain to peel off a part of its facing. They therefore adopted the practice of inserting large stones in the midst of pebbles, thereby giving it a somewhat more solid and certainly more picturesque appearance (Plate XIX). This may be called the " diaper-pebble " style. The large apsidal temple at Harwan is built of this kind of masonry. It is, however, worthy of note that in this temple the diaper-pebble facing was covered with a revetment of beautiful and elaborately moulded bricks, some of which are still *in situ* on the enclosure wall.

This style was followed at Harwan by the diaper-rubble masonry (Plate XVI), which is represented by a large stupa, its surrounding walls, and chapels. The discovery of a coin of Toramana underneath the stairs of the stupa fixes its date, and consequently also the style in which it is built, as that of the sixth century A.D. or later. This kind of masonry is also found in a building at Parihasapura, where it may possibly be nearly contemporary with the buildings of Lalitaditya (eighth century A.D.).

MEDIÆVAL ARCHITECTURE (A.D. 600 TO 1300)

Buddhist Buildings

We now come to the well-known and much described architecture of mediæval Kashmir. It may be said with a fair amount of accuracy to begin at about the sixth to seventh centuries A.D. It ended with the transfer of the kingdom from Hindu to Muslim hands in A.D. 1337, though probably small monolithic shrines, such as those of Patan (Plate LVII) and Koil, continued to be consecrated even after that time. The buildings which represent this style may conveniently be divided into two classes—namely, the Buddhist and the Brahmanical. In point of materials, ornament, and technique, there is practically no difference between the two, but the religious needs of the two communities being in certain essentials different, they differ widely in plan and elevation. The Buddhists, who inherited a long artistic tradition, naturally adhered to their old models, though they employed better materials and somewhat elaborated the decoration. The material brought into use was a beautiful grey limestone, which was easy to carve, and presented a very smooth surface when properly dressed. The plinth of the old stupa, which was a simple rectangular structure with a single flight of steps, was now elaborated into a square with one or more offsets on each side projecting far into the courtyard (Plate LV), and flanked on either hand by side walls adorned with sculptural reliefs. The plinth in the larger buildings consisted of a double terrace, each comprising five courses of finely chiselled stone blocks of great size. The two lowest courses and the fourth course were plain, the third was fashioned into a round torus moulding, and the topmost into a filleted torus or cyma recta. The re-entering angles of the offsets afforded a pleasing contrast of light and shade.

As there is not a single stupa of which the drum remains intact, it is difficult to say precisely what its external decorations were.

Of the monasteries there is little to be said, as only one example survives—namely, the Rajavihara of Parihasapura. In plan it is a cellular quadrangle facing a rectangular courtyard. The cells were preceded by an open verandah. In the middle of one side was the flight of steps which afforded an entrance and exit. The central cell on this side served as the vestibule. In the range of cells on the opposite side are a set of more spacious rooms which served either as a refectory or as the abbot's private apartments. Externally, and probably internally also, the walls were plain. The roof was probably sloping, and gabled like modern roofs in Kashmir.

Parihasapura has also bequeathed to us the only surviving example of a Buddhist chaitya, or temple. It is a square chamber built upon a square base similar to that of the stupa, save for the offsets and three stairs, and is enclosed by a plain wall, with entrance facing the temple stairs. The stairs lead up to the portico which gave admission to the sanctum. The latter was an open chamber surrounded on all sides by a narrow corridor which served as a circumambulatory path. At the four corners of the sanctum are bases of pillars which no doubt held some sort of screen designed partly to conceal the Holy of Holies from profane eyes. As the external wall of the corridor has been almost razed to the ground, it is very difficult to say whether there were openings in it for admission of light and air; probably there were.

The portico was covered by a massive trefoil arch, which in its turn might have been surmounted by a pedimental roof. The roof of the shrine was probably pyramidal like that of contemporary Hindu temples. At any rate, its plan would easily admit of such a roof.

Hindu Buildings

The second and far most numerous group of buildings belonging to this style are Hindu temples. The earliest example of this class, the date of which can be fixed through archæological as well as literary evidence, is the temple of Martand (Plate LIII), which is also the greatest and one of the most finished of all the Kashmir temples. From this, however, it must not be inferred that the mediæval Hindu architecture of Kashmir was born like Athene in panoply fully accoutred and complete to the last detail; that, in other words, it was evolved by a single brain or set of brains at a specified point of time. It is true that, owing to the remarkable dearth of early dated examples, we are reduced to mere conjecture as to what was the prototype, and what were the stages of evolution which resulted in such magnificent products of the builder's art as the Martand and Avantisvami temples (Plates LIII, XLVIII, and XLIX). But it seems reasonable to presume that the earlier examples were simpler, and that art progressed step by step, up to a certain point, from the simple to the more elaborate.

We have briefly noticed above the extent and depth of the influence of the Buddhist art of Gandhara on that of Kashmir. So great was it that it would be more correct to say that, excepting the natural and unavoidable difference in the material used, the two are practically identical. Though the religious needs of the Hindus did not necessitate their borrowing stupas and *sangharamas* from the Buddhists, such considerations did not lie in the way of their taking advantage of the experience the latter had gained in temple-building. The needs of the two communities were the same in two respects: a chamber was required for installation of a divine image (whether of the Buddha and the Bodhisattva or of Vishnu and any other Hindu deity is of little importance), and accommodation was required for worshippers. It is of course not impossible for a new religion to commence an architecture of its own, but the chances are overwhelming in favour of its utilising, at least in the initial stages, the older models, and adapting them to its purposes. This may not always hold good in the case where the new religion follows in the wake of foreign conquest and the conquerors have already evolved a style of their own, which they naturally wish to impose upon the vanquished. But when the new religion, like the old, is indigenous; when both live in mutual amity and exchange of good offices; and, lastly, when the mode of worship of both is practically the same, it becomes almost inevitable that the sacred buildings of the new religion should follow the style of those of the older one. This, at any rate, has happened twice in Kashmir, once when Buddhism slowly and gradually gave way to Hinduism, and again when, with the accession of Shah Mir, Islam, at first imperceptibly, but with increasing speed, supplanted Hinduism in the valley.[1]

Regarding the first transformation, the similarity pointed out by Foucher[2] between the "angular roofed" vihara (*le Vihara à toit anguleux*) of Gandhara and the temples of Kashmir, particularly the larger temple at Loduv (Plate XLVII), is specially interesting and instructive. The latter is an extremely plain structure, circular in plan internally, square externally, very simple in construction, and almost devoid of decoration. It has a single opening, the entrance, which is arched at the top. The arch is semicircular and built of horizontal projecting courses. The few stones of the roof which still exist prove that it was steep, straight, and sloped. The stones of which it is built are comparatively small in size. This is a curious feature, considering that the quarry which probably supplied the gigantic blocks of the Avantipur temple, and from which stones of immense size are still taken, is little more than a stone's throw from the shrine. This may be merely coincidence; but, taking it in conjunction with the simplicity of its design, it seems probable that the temple belongs to the time when the great possibilities of ashlar-dressed limestone began first to dawn upon the architects of Kashmir—that is, to the sixth or seventh century A.D.[3]

This hypothesis is strengthened by the striking resemblance of the Loduv (Plate XLVII) temple to the vihara of Guniyar in the Swat

[1] On the latter occasions, the Muslims, like their co-religionists in India, borrowed the materials and the technique of the Hindu shrines, but, unlike them, retained the form of the Hindu temple as far as it was compatible with their religious requirements.

[2] *L'Art Gréco-Bouddhique du Gandhara*, tome I.

[3] As far as our present knowledge extends, the materials commonly used for religious buildings in Kashmir in the earlier centuries of the Christian era (say up to the fifth-sixth centuries A.D.) were chips, pebbles and rubble stones—*e.g.* at Ushkar and Harwan. By the middle of the eighth century, the time of the Martand temple, the Kashmiris knew all that there was to be known about the architectural use of limestone.

valley. The description of the former which has been given above would literally apply to the latter but for a few minor differences, which are: in the Guniyar example the plainness of the cella is relieved internally by four recesses placed diagonally; the row of projecting brackets which support the eaves of the roof are replaced at Loduv by a simple cornice consisting of three courses of projecting filleted blocks; on the other hand, there is no trace of a pediment over the entrance of the vihara. These details, however, do not impair the analogy between the two. Now the Guniyar structure cannot possibly be later than the fifth century A.D., and unless there is something positive to prove the lateness of the Loduv temple (to my knowledge there is nothing), we must on the strength of the reasons adduced above consider it either contemporaneous with the former, or at most a century or so later.

A structure of which the date has caused much controversy is the Śankaracharya temple (Plate V) on the Takht-i-Sulaiman hill. General Cunningham, relying mainly upon local tradition, assigned[1] it to Jalauka, son of Asoka, whom he puts about 220 B.C.

Professor Bühler denies the existence of this tradition, but does not himself give any definite opinion. Mr. Fergusson rejected Cunningham's view chiefly on grounds of style.[2] He remarks: "At the bottom of the steps is a round-headed doorway, not, it is true, such as is universal in the Hindu imitations of Muslim architecture in the seventeenth and eighteenth centuries. The same is the case in the small temples alongside, which are evidently of the same age. The one most like it that I am acquainted with is that erected by Chait Singh of Benares (1770-1781) at Ramnagar at the end of the eighteenth century. I know of no straight lined pyramid of much older date than that, and no temple with a polygonal plan combined with a circular cell, as is the case here, that is of ancient date. The ceil itself with the linga is undoubtedly modern, and the four pillars in the cell with the

---

[1] *J.A.S.B.*, 1848, ii, p. 247 *et seqq.*
[2] Fergusson, vol. i, p. 254 *et seqq.*

Persian inscriptions upon them are avowedly of the seventeenth century. It is suggested, moreover, that they belong to a repair. My own conviction, however, is that the temple, as it now stands, was commenced by some nameless Hindus in honour of Śiva during the tolerant reign of Jahangir and that the building was stopped at the date engraved on the staircase, A.H. 1069 (A.D. 1659), the first year of Aurangzeb. It was then unfinished, and has remained a ruin, and this may have given it an ancient appearance, but not such as to justify putting its date back 1870 years."

Sir Aurel Stein is inclined to accept the opinion of Fergusson, at least so far as the superstructure is concerned. He states that "the circular cella, which contains a modern linga, was undoubtedly built in Muslim times. The imposing polygonal base, consisting of re-markably massive blocks and without mortar, must belong to a much earlier period (Plate LXXIV). Whatever may be the date and origin of the temple on the Takht hill, its connection with the worship of Jyestharudra is highly probable."[1]

Cunningham's theory, which was based on the traditional identity of the temple with the temple of Jalauka, lost all basis when the existence of that tradition was questioned and disproved. Fergus-son's arguments in support, on the one hand, of his rejection of Cunningham's view and, on the other, of the plausibility of his own, are equally untenable for the following reasons:

1. True round-headed arches of the early Hindu times are known in India; and the existence, therefore, of a horizontal round-headed arch in a Hindu temple does not necessarily imply its late date and imitation from Muslim models. At Loduv we have a similar arch.

2. Whatever the value of his assertion that he did not know of any straight-lined pyramid much older than the eighteenth century, nor any "temple with a polygonal plan combined with a circular cella," his deduction from it is invalidated by the fact that the Śankaracharya temple is not a straight-lined pyramid in the sense which his words

[1] *Raiat.*, vol. ii, p. 290.

seemingly imply, and that its plan is not polygonal. Its walls rise straight up to the eaves, and its roof, the lowest course only of which is extant, was triangular in section like the roofs of other ancient temples in Kashmir. In plan the cella is externally square, with a couple of offsets on each side.

3. Though the pillars in the sanctum bearing Persian inscriptions are modern and were probably put up in Shah Jahan's time, it does not seem that they alter the position in any way, for the ancient domical ceiling built of concentric circles of *kanjur* masonry is still in existence above the modern ceiling.

4. Lastly, his conviction that it was begun by some nameless Hindus in Jahangir's time and was left incomplete after the accession of Aurangzeb in A.D. 1659, "which gives it its ancient look," is flatly contradicted by Bernier, who saw it in A.D. 1664, only five years later, and states that it was in ruins and desuetude. Catrou, whose *General History of the Mughal Empire* was published in 1708, only one year after Aurangzeb's death, ascribes it to Solomon. This shows that its origin was even then unknown, which would scarcely be the case if its construction had been taken in hand in the time of Jahangir and stopped by Aurangzeb's order.

Rai Bahadur Daya Ram Sahni states that "the temple belongs to the same mediæval period as all the other buildings of this class,"[1] which is probably correct. But his further remark, "that the enclosure wall of this temple represents a decadent form of the cellular peristyle,"[2] seems to imply that the smallness (that is what he probably means by decadence) of the peristyle necessarily connotes a late date, and that consequently the Śankaracharya temple is later than those temples which have larger peristyles. Now there are several temples in Kashmir whose date admits of no doubt—*e.g.*, the Martand, the Avantipur, the Patan, the Kother temples. The first belongs to the beginning of the eighth century A.D. and the last to the end of the eleventh century. But the lapse of the three centuries and more does

---

[1] A.S.R., 1915-16, p. 55.   [2] *Op. cit.*, p. 54.

not appear to have in any way influenced the dimensions of the peristyle, except of course in cases where the reduced size of the central shrine itself necessitated proportionate reduction in the dimensions of the peristyle also, and secondly where the nature of the site chosen for the erection of the temple did not permit of the construction of a large, or for the matter of that any, peristyle. The first, for instance, is the case in the two Patan temples which were built by Śankaravarman and his queen Sugandha at one and the same time. The Pandrethan temple which, I believe, belongs to the middle of the twelfth century A.D., but which according to Rai Bahadur Daya Ram Sahni " is certainly quite 200 years older," has a surrounding wall, but no cellular peristyle; this would be very strange indeed in a temple which so closely followed the Avantisvami temple (A.D. 852-855), if the peristyle were an indispensable adjunct to the early Hindu temples. As a matter of fact we know from extant examples that it was not. It has been established that the two larger temples at Wangath were built by Lalitaditya, who built the Martand temple also. Of these three temples erected by the same king, one (Martand) has the largest peristyle known to exist in Kashmir, the second (Jyeshtheśa at Wangath) has a comparatively small one, and the third (Bhuteśa at Wangath) has none at all. Thus it seems to me that the smallness—the so-called decadence—of the peristyle, or its very absence, does not in itself afford any indication of the age of the temples.

From the foregoing remarks it will have been observed that though it may be indisputable that the Śankaracharya temple " belongs to the same mediæval period as all the buildings of this class," its proper position in the sequence of Kashmir monuments is by no means well established. Fortunately in this matter the temple itself comes to our aid. The salient features of the central shrine are the following: (1) externally it is square in plan with two offsets on each side; (2) internally it is circular; (3) the cella is absolutely without decoration both internally and externally; (4) it is pierced by a single narrow opening (the entrance) semicircular at the top and surmounted by a very shallow and steep pediment; (5) it stands in a narrow octagonal court which is enclosed by a low parapet wall adorned with rows of small niches.   Of all the temples in Kashmir that to which it bears the closest resemblance, both in disposition of parts and in ornament (or rather the want of it), is the one at Loduv.   Apart from the enclosure wall and the base, which are submerged in the swamps formed by the spring at Loduv, and which therefore are not available for comparison, the only difference between the two shrines is that the Śankaracharya has two offsets on each side externally, while the other has none.   This certainly is an innovation and an improvement, since the light and shade of the re-entering angles of the offsets compares favourably with the baldness of the exterior of the Loduv temple. But it must be noticed that the offsets are severely plain.   In this respect they stand in very marked contrast with other examples of mediæval Hindu architecture.   Not only do such undoubtedly late temples as those of Mamal and Kother possess more or less ornate trefoiled recesses on each side, but even the very latest miniature monolithic shrines, which were probably erected at the time when Hindu rule and Hindu art were at a low level, display these decorative features, sometimes actually carved out of the stone, as in the structural examples, or merely traced in outline.   It seems, therefore, clear that the absence of such decorative features as attained currency in the eighth century is, in case of the Śankaracharya temple, an indication of its older age, and not a sign of decadence.   In other words, though the Śankaracharya temple is somewhat later than the Loduv temple, it cannot be less than a century older than the Martand temple; that is to say, its approximate date is probably A.D. 700.

The octagonal enclosure is more a matter of accident than of design.   It is due to the situation of the temple, which precluded the possibility of a larger enclosure of any other type without immense expenditure.   But notwithstanding the fact that it is a great improvement upon the Loduv temple, there is a considerable gap from the

Śankaracharya to the Martand which must have taken a good deal of time and invention to bridge over.

In accelerating progress, however, Lalitaditya's large resources and even-handed generosity to the Hindus and the Buddhists effectively came to the aid of the Kashmir architect. To the Buddhist the king's bounty brought no change. All that he did was to use better and more massive materials. He built a monastery of gigantic ashlar-dressed limestone blocks exactly as he would have built it of rubble stone and timber. The Hindu, on the other hand, used both his hands and his brain, with what result is evident to every one who has seen the wonderful ruins of the Martand temple. He did not invent many new forms of design and decoration. He simply re-arranged the motifs he had ready at hand into a new artistic combination which was so beautiful and at the same time so dignified that it fixed for all succeeding centuries of Hindu rule the ideal of what a temple of the Gods should be. He had already adapted a Buddhist temple for his purpose at Loduv; he had improved it by the addition of offsets at Śankaracharya; he had pierced the offsets with trefoiled niches at Narastan (Plate LII), which probably follows Śankaracharya in date. The most important feature that still remained to be added was the cellular quadrangle. This he achieved at Martand.[1]

Regarding the origin of the cellular quadrangle there can be little doubt. The Buddhist monastery from very early times consisted of a quadrangular block of rooms facing a common courtyard, in which usually stood a small private chapel. If the chapel was a large one and placed in the centre of the court, the plan would exactly correspond with that of the Martand or the Avantisvami temple, the former of which is contemporary with the Buddhist structures of Parihasapura. Of course, in the Hindu temples the size of the cells was considerably reduced, as they were no longer required for residential purposes, but merely for the accommodation of the images;

---

[1] I do not mean to say positively that the cellular quadrangle was for the first time used at Martand ; but only that it is the earliest dated example of which we have knowledge.

the width of the promenade in front of the cells was also reduced in the temple; the columns which supported its roofs were now used for a purely decorative purpose, and sometimes, when the resources of the builders failed, were altogether given up; the unpretentious flight of steps, quite suitable for a congregation of religious mendicants, was replaced by a magnificent double-chambered entrance, almost equal in size to the temple, to make it a fit portal for an abode of the Gods. These and other details, as the necessity or the fancy of the artist dictated, were gradually added; but the broad outline of the ordinary Hindu temple of the best period remained the same—namely, a chaitya built in the middle of a monastic courtyard.

Later, when the Hindu rule lost its early vigour and the country was constantly torn by intestine warfare, the religious buildings of Kashmir gradually lost much of their impressive grandeur. Architectural features, such as the trefoil arch and the detached column, lost their original purpose and became mere decorative motifs. The dimensions of the temple gradually dwindled until they became small monolithic miniatures not more than 2 feet each way. The column was altogether given up. The arch became shallower and shallower. At Payar (Plate LI) it is merely a sculptured niche over the lintel of a rectangular doorway; at the Bumazu cave-temple only its outline has been shown; the small shrine in the Patan (Plate LVII) spring does not show it at all, though it still reproduces the elaborate double pediment and the moulded bases and capitals of the jambs. Thus, curiously enough, the principal features of both the beginning and the end of the mediæval Hindu architecture of Kashmir are the absence of the structural trefoil arch and the colonnade, which would for the purpose of fixing their chronological sequences be confusing enough, were it not that other characteristics such as the design, decoration, mouldings, etc., render it possible to distinguish one from the other.

The mediæval architecture of Kashmir depended for its effect upon (1) the simplicity and unity of its design, (2) the massiveness of the blocks of limestone and granite that were used, (3) the finish of dressing, and (4) last but not least, the natural beauty of the site chosen for erection of the temple. Its main feature is a happy combination of the column and the arch.

(1) The temple was conceived as a single whole, and after its construction afforded little or no scope for subsequent additions. Its plan and disposition were apparent at a single glance. In this characteristic it differed essentially from the majority of Indian temples, which, whatever their beauty in detail, present when viewed as a whole a rather confused appearance.

(2) and (3). All the temples of Kashmir, except those of Wangath (Plate LXII) and Buniar (Plate LX), in which the material used is granite, are built of limestone, which the quarries of Loduv, Zewan, and Ajas plentifully supply. The blocks used are extraordinarily massive, often measuring 10 feet and more in length. The floor of the chaitya at Parihasapura consists of a single block approximately $14 \times 12 \times 6$ feet. The blocks, before being placed in their proper position, were only roughly dressed, the architectural decoration and sculptured reliefs being merely blocked out; the final dressing was done *in situ*. It was an inconvenient and somewhat circuitous method, but it was necessary, as otherwise the delicate carving, if not done *in situ*, might sustain grievous damage in handling. Lime mortar was undoubtedly used; but the stability of the masonry was sufficiently assured by the massiveness of the blocks, which had only vertical pressure to resist, there being no lateral thrust, owing to the absence of voussoir arches and the frequent use of iron clamps. There is reason to believe that this wealth of stone carving was covered by a coat of gypsum plaster, which was probably painted, and in which the more delicate details of sculpture and other decoration were finished off.

(4) A natural result of the pantheistic tendencies of early Brahmanism is the extraordinary reverence in which both the Buddhists and the Hindus have always held Nature. To them the wide prospect

over the rolling plains, as at Ellura, or the wild grandeur of glaciers and eternal snows, as at Amarnath, or the view of a magnificent sunset over the hills, as at Martand, not only made a general æsthetic appeal, but had a special religious significance; for they viewed Nature as the multifold manifestation of the Almighty. It was for this reason that they invariably chose the most naturally beautiful spots for their sanctuaries. Much of the charm which the religious buildings of Kashmir undoubtedly possess is due to this fact. To take only one example: as the site of a temple, the conical summit of the Takht-i-Sulaiman hill, rising a thousand feet vertically above the surrounding plains and commanding a panoramic view of the entire mountain-girdled valley, would be difficult to rival anywhere. The temple seems the natural apex of the pyramidal hill. The steep sombre lines of the barren slopes blend insensibly with the still more sombre, grey, and vertical lines of the temple walls. Art has not only advantageously utilised, but also emphasised, the natural characteristics of the situation (Plates IV and V).

PLAN.—In plan the Kashmirian temple (Plates LXVIII, LXXIII, and LXXV) is a rectangular quadrangle pierced with cells facing the courtyard. The temple usually consists of a single chamber with a portico, and is, as a rule, at the point of intersection of the diagonals of the courtyard. The entrance, which is almost equal in dimensions to the main shrine, is a double-chambered structure, and is built in the middle of a shorter side of the peristyle. The chambers are divided by a partition wall, which is open in the middle and was probably closed by wooden doors. The entrance has a double flight of steps, one external and the other facing the temple. The stairs are flanked with plain stone rails and sculptured sidewalls.

The main shrine consists, as has been stated above, of a single square chamber, preceded by a small portico (Plate LXV). Externally a facet is added on each side, which is hollowed out into a trefoil-arched niche; the front one, being open, serves as entrance to the sanctum. The temple stands on a single or double base which consists usually of five ashlar-dressed courses, the first, the second, and the fourth of which are plain and the remaining two moulded (Plate LXXIV, A, B, C, and D).

The cells of the peristyle also stand on a plinth which is similar to the base of the temple. The central cell on each of three sides is slightly larger than the rest, and is somewhat advanced beyond the line of the peristyle.

Some of the temples possess subsidiary shrines. They are usually built in an angle of the courtyard and are similar in plan to the main shrine (Plate LXVIII).

VARIATIONS IN PLAN.—The Loduv and the Śankaracharya temples are circular in plan internally. The former does not possess any facets externally, and in the latter they have not yet developed into trefoiled niches. The Payar and some other temples do not possess any cellular peristyle. The Narastan temple has a plain enclosure wall with a gateway of the conventional type. It has a small tank in front, and a bath chamber in one of the corners of the enclosure wall. The Śankaracharya temple has an octagonal range of miniature cells in its surrounding wall.

WALLS.—The walls are built of finely dressed and massive blocks of limestone. Mortar was used, though not in considerable quantities, as the stones were secured by iron clamps. The joints are usually very thin. The surface was often carved with sculptured reliefs, geometrical and floral patterns, but the internal surface of the walls of the cella was generally kept plain. The walls were surmounted by a sloping cornice, usually decorated with rows of geese alternating with rosettes and *kīrtimukhas* (Plate LXX). Externally, the walls of the peristyle are plain, except in certain cases where a series of shallow projections marks the position of the cross-walls of the cells. Internally the pilasters of the cells are decorated with half-engaged columns carved in low relief (Plate LXXII).

OPENINGS.—Curiously enough there exist no traces whatever of any windows or skylights in any of the known temples of the valley.

This is probably due mainly to the fact that the light and air entering through a single large doorway was enough for a small square cella.[1] Still less was there any need for such apertures in the case of the cells of the peristyle. The only openings, therefore, that are found in the walls of the Kashmirian temples are the doorways. They were rectangular, surmounted by trefoil arches, and were usually preceded by trefoiled and pedimented porticoes. In the Loduv and Śankaracharya temples, the entrances are round-headed.

Temples of the *maṇḍapa*, or " bower " type, like the Pandrethan (Plate XLIV) and Payar (Plate LI) temples, being open on all four sides, have naturally four doorways; while temples of the *vimāna* type, such as the Avantisvami temple, have only one entrance.

A large temple (Bhuteśa) in the group A at Wangath has two doorways facing each other.

Ceilings.—Ceilings of Kashmiri temples were of four types, or rather three only, the third being merely a variety of the second type.

1. The ceiling of superimposed diminishing squares. The plan of the cells being square, the architect chose the method of cutting off the angles as the easiest means of spanning it. The second square thus formed was further reduced by another series of four stone beams which rested upon the first four. This process was repeated until a single square stone of sufficient dimensions was found to span the whole gap at the top. The triangular spaces resulting from this construction were filled with carved figures of flying Yakshas, and the apex was usually decorated with a full-blown lotus flower. The best example of this kind of ceiling is in the temple at Pandrethan (Plate LXVI).

2. The domical ceiling. The dome rested upon a projecting string-course, and was built of *kanjur* or *kanait*, a light and porous limestone which burns into excellent lime. It was not built on the radiating principle, but consisted of a series of concentric circles of

---

[1] The temple at Saidabad in Bhimber, which is situated in a very hot place, does possess ventilation apertures.

small blocks of *kanjur* held together by mortar of extraordinarily adhesive properties. The stability of the dome, in fact, depended entirely upon the tenacity of the mortar. The ancient architects probably constructed this dome much as a modern engineer would construct an arch of cement concrete. The two largest temples at Wangath have ceilings of this type.

3. The corbelled ceiling seems to have been a variety of the domical ceiling, the only difference being that in this case the dome instead of rising direct from the string-course is supported on an elaborate system of corbelled pendentives. The corbels could have also been used with great advantage in the ceilings of the first type, inasmuch as they were capable of sustaining a greater weight than the unsupported stone beams, and could more easily reduce the span of the space to be covered.

4. The fourth type may aptly be described as the " no-ceiling " type. The best known, perhaps the only, examples of this class are the buildings at Narastan and Naranthal. The walls of the cella are carried up vertically until they reach the level of the eaves. Therefrom the pyramidal roof itself forms the ceiling.

5. A small temple at Wangath and the detached room to the north-west of the Śankaracharya temple have flat ceilings of rectangular stone slabs resting on transverse stone beams supported by columns.

Roofs.—The roofs are invariably pyramidal. In the examples which have survived—*e.g.*, the Pandrethan (Plate XLIV), Payar (Plate LI), and Manasbal (Plate LXI) temples, not to mention the miniature shrines at Patan (Plate LVII), Koil, etc.—the pyramid is a double one, the lower storey being truncated at about the middle of the roof, and a second one built on a projecting string-course. The apex of the pediments of the porches reaches up to the upper edge of the lower storey, and produces a pleasing effect of light and shade. The plainness of the upper pyramid is sometimes relieved by a miniature gabled trefoil niche (Plate XLIV) in the middle of each of the four sides. The apex of the roof, as well as that of the four pediments, was crowned with a ribbed melon-like finial. Two of these are extant at Payar (Plate LI).

The roof of the small temple at Naranthal consists of a single plain pyramid.

COLUMNS.—Perhaps the most striking feature of the Kashmiri temple is the majestic colonnade (Plates XLVIII, LIII, and LX) which surrounds it on all sides. The columns are either smooth or fluted, and at the angles of the peristyle they are square. They are composed of three separate parts : the base, the shaft, and the capital. The base is either a plain square block with the upper edge rounded off, as at Avantipur (Plate XLIX), or is elaborately moulded, as at Martand (Plate LIII) and elsewhere. The latter has been described by Cunningham thus : " The upper member is an ovolo with a straight fillet above, and the apophyge below. The next is a filleted torus, with a fillet above and below and surmounting the straight face or neck of the pillar. In the large Martand pillar the torus is plain. Beneath this is a quirked ovolo with a straight fillet above and below, and the last is the plinth. In all these the upper and lower members are of the same height; that is, the ovolo and the apophyge are equal to the plinth."

When the shafts are fluted the flutes are sometimes so shallow as to have scarcely any concavity. In some cases—for example, at Avantipur—the central portion of the flute is roughly chiselled, and is in strong contrast to the edges, which are finely dressed. In the columns of the Patan temples the flutes are well accentuated. The number of flutes in different examples is twelve, sixteen, twenty, and twenty-four; but never less than twelve nor more than twenty-four.

It is difficult to say whether or not the diameter of the columns was a factor in determining its height.

The capitals are square, voluted, or bracketed, and rest upon a ribbed astragal (Plate LXVII). The height of the capital is usually equal to the upper diameter of the column. The bracket capital is sometimes adorned with figures of Yakshas.

The inter-columniation of the Kashmir colonnade was about two-thirds of the height of the column itself.

The entablature consists of the architrave and the cornice. In the case of the peristyle, the architrave returns, connecting the pillar with the pilaster of the cell behind. Both the architrave and the cornice are decorated with rows of rosettes alternating with *kīrtimukhas* or grinning lions' heads (Plates LXX, A, and LXXIV, E).

ORNAMENT.—This consists of sculptured figures and geometrical and floral patterns which are mostly intermingled (Plates LXVII, LXX, LXXI, and LXXII). The most common motif of the former is the figure of a god or goddess standing in a pedimented niche (Plates LI and LXIV). At Avantipur there are groups of figures of both sexes, engaged in drinking, making love, or other occupations (Plate L). The sculptured reliefs are principally found on the walls of the entrance and the flank walls of the stairs. It is probable, as stated above, that not only the plain wall surfaces but also the reliefs were covered with a fine coat of lime plaster, on which the addition of colour defined the more delicate details of decoration.

The principal mouldings (Plate LXXIV) employed are (1) cyma recta, (2) torus, (3) filleted torus, (4) ovolo, (5) echinus, and (6) fillet. None of these was enriched by any surface decoration, except in the case of the second, which was in a few examples adorned with broad, plain, slanting bands carved in bold relief.

MUSLIM ARCHITECTURE

(FOURTEENTH CENTURY A.D. AND ONWARDS)

It will have been remarked, from the short account of Kashmir history given above, that the transfer of the sceptre from the Hindus to the Muslims was a purely domestic matter, and had nothing to do with the great Pan-Islamic conquests of the twelfth and thirteenth centuries. It was, moreover, an entirely secular affair. Rinchana, who was the first non-Hindu to occupy the Kashmir throne, was a Tibetan, and became a Muslim by accident. Shah Mir's usurpation was a coup d'état and not a conquest. He and his immediate successors depended upon the support of the indigenous nobles, who were mostly Hindus, for the stability of their rule. The absence from Kashmir of the regular Saracenic mosques with cloisters and domes is not therefore surprising. The Muslims in Kashmir were in the beginning far too few to initiate an architecture of their own. All that they did was to utilise the materials of disused Hindu temples for construction of their mosques. The result was peculiar. The most characteristic examples of this style are the mosque of Madin Sahib, outside the Sangin Darwaza of the Hari Parbat fort and its adjacent ruins, the ruins of the mosques on the roadside at Vitsarnag, and Zain-ul-abidin's mosque on the island in the Wular lake. All these will be described in detail below.

Another structure belonging to this period, and fundamentally different from all other buildings in Kashmir, is the tomb of Zain-ul-abidin's mother (Plate VIII). The plinth originally belonged to a Hindu or Buddhist shrine, and does not seem to have been tampered with by the Muslim architect, who simply followed the lines laid down by his Hindu predecessor. A peculiar feature of the brick buildings of this period (there are only three: the tomb of Zain-ul-abidin's mother, Madin Sahib's tomb, and the anonymous tomb on the island in the Wular) is the glazed tile-work with which they were decorated.

" The mosques and tombs of the modern Kashmiri style are so similar that their features need not be separately discussed. The tombs are square in plan. The mosques are either self-contained, square buildings like the tombs : such are the mosques of Madani, Shah Hamadan (where the cloisters were added later) (Plate VI), and the Jama' Masjid at Pampur (Plate XLVI); or else they consist of a group of square-planned buildings connected together by a colonnade like the Jama' Masjid in Srinagar.

" The walls are constructed sometimes of bricks and mortar, sometimes of logs laid across each other, the space between logs being in some cases filled with brick-work. Piers are constructed of timber in the same way.

" In large chambers where the timbers of the roof or ceiling require intermediate support, modern columns are used with very good effect. Sometimes these columns are elaborately ornamented, and there is a tendency in modern restoration, as, for instance, at the mosque of Naqshband, to cover the bases with coarse and unsuitable ornament. Timber trusses do not seem to have been understood by ancient builders, but they are now employed in restoration. The old method of supporting the rafters was by building up piers formed of logs laid horizontally—a very extravagant arrangement. The typical roof covering consists of turf laid in birch bark, which retains waterproof properties for a great number of years. The birch bark is laid on boards, and these in turn are supported on rafters. The roof is usually surmounted by a steeple, the finial of which is moulded, the largest moulding being sometimes in the shape of an outspread umbrella usually covered with metal. All the older buildings appear either to have lost their steeples and finials, or to have had them restored. The oldest umbrella mouldings are probably some of those on the Jama' Masjid (Plates IX and X) at Srinagar, erected in the reign of Aurangzeb.

" A remarkable feature in the steeple is the sloping gable which projects from the sides. Window openings and balustrades are commonly filled with elaborate *jālī* screens, the patterns of which are formed by little pieces of wood fitted together so as to form geometrical patterns (Plate X).

" The angles of the eaves are generally ornamented with wooden pendants suspended from the corners, carved like small bells and shaped like cactus leaves. The cornices are very heavy, and are formed of logs corbelled out from the wall face on timbers laid crosswise. The butt ends of the cross timbers form a dentil course, and the space between them is filled with elaborate carving. The best examples are at the mosques of Madani at Srinagar and of Amir at Pampur.

"The interior of the mosque of Shah Hamadan is entirely covered with panelling consisting of geometrical patterns.

"The mouldings are as a rule flat, not deeply recessed, and curved and hollow members seem to be avoided. They generally consist of flat fillets, each of which is differently carved.

"The carved ornament is generally Saracenic in character. In older buildings the patterns are conventional. In some later restorations realistic flowers are carved, bearing much resemblance to the stone-work of Shah Jahan in the Taj at Agra and elsewhere.

"Of the Mughal style as exemplified by buildings in Kashmir it is not necessary to say much, because the style is practically the same as that with which we are familiar at Agra, Delhi, and Lahore. . . . The Pathar Masjid (Plate VII), the mosque of Akhun Mulla Shah (Plate XII), and the largest barahdari in Shalimar Bagh (Plate XIV) are unsurpassed in purity of style and perfection of detail by any buildings in Agra or Delhi.

"Another important branch of architecture in which the Mughals excelled, and in which they left their mark upon Srinagar, is gardening. These gardens conform strictly to the style of Shalamar Bagh at Lahore and Delhi, and other gardens of the same period in India; but nowhere is there to be found a group comprising so many examples as at Srinagar."[1]

---

[1] The quotations given above regarding the Muslim architecture of Kashmir are from Nicholls' article in the *Archæological Survey of India Report* for the year 1906-7.

IV

MONUMENTS IN SRINAGAR AND ITS VICINITY

From	To	Distance.	Mode of Travelling.	Remarks.
Srinagar	Śankaracharya temple	2½ miles.	By carriage to the Mission Hospital and thence on foot	
	Patthar Masjid Shah Hamadan's Mosque Zain - ul - abidin's enclosure Jama' Masjid Hari Parbat Mosque of Madin Sahib Vitsar Nag		By boat to Badshah and thence by carriage to Jama' Masjid, or throughout by carriage	3 to 4 hours
	Chashma-i-Shahi	5½ miles by motor road from Srinagar		
	Pari Ma hal and back	1½ miles on foot from Chashmai Shahi		Srinagar to Harwan by road is 11½ miles
	Nishat	2½ miles by motor road		
	Shalimar	2 miles by motor road		
	Harwan	1½ miles by motor road		

ŚANKARACHARYA TEMPLE

The Śankaracharya temple is situated on the summit of the Takht-i-Sulaiman hill, to the south-east of Srinagar (Plate IV). Neither the hill nor the temple preserves its ancient name; in Hindu times the former bore the name of Gopadri, and the latter—or more probably some earlier structure which occupied its place—that of Jyesh-theśvara. But the modern name of the hill seems to be of fairly long standing, as it is mentioned by Catrou,[1] and in a slightly altered form (Koh-i-Sulaiman) by Abul Fazl.[2] The temple is built on a high octagonal plinth approached by a long flight of steps enclosed by two side-walls which originally bore two Persian inscriptions. One of these was dated A.H. 1069=A.D. 1659. Both inscriptions disappeared some time in the last few decades. The plinth is surmounted by a low parapet wall 23' 6" long on each side, the inner surface of which was originally adorned by a range of eighty-four round-headed recesses enclosed in rectangular panels. The greater part of the wall has now fallen. The shrine consists of a cell, circular inside, with a diameter of 13' 2". Externally it is square with two projecting facets on each side (Plate V). The surface is plain, except for the salient and re-entering angles of the facets. The maximum thickness of the walls in the middle of each facet is 8' 2". The interior of the sanctum is covered by a modern ceiling " composed of flat stone slabs and wooden boards, which rest on two lintels of the same material, themselves supported on four columns in the centre of the room. The south-west column bears two Persian inscriptions, one of which states that the column on which it is engraved was carved by a mason named Bihishti in the year 54—i.e., A.H. 1054, corresponding to A.D. 1644. The date falls in the reign of Shah Jahan. It is obvious, therefore, that this ceiling with its columns was erected in the time of that king."[3] The original ceiling, which this modern addition has hidden from view, is dome-shaped and built of horizontal courses of *kanait* or *kanjur* (a kind of light and porous limestone). The absence of the tre-foiled entrance to the sanctum, and similar niches on the other

---

[1] *General History of the Mughal Empire*, Calcutta edition, p. 196.   It was originally published in 1708.

[2] *Ain-i-Akbari*, tr. Jarrett, vol. ii, p. 355.

[3] A.S.R., 1915-16, p. 72.

three sides, is remarkable. In this respect, as in the circular interior plan, this temple is similar to the larger temple at Loduv. The brick roof seems to have been constructed within the last century.

The date of this temple has been a source of controversy among archæologists. General Cunningham and, after him, Lieut. Cole assigned it to the times of Jalauka (whom they date 220 B.C.) on the strength of local tradition. This theory has been rejected, firstly on architectural grounds, and secondly because of the doubtful character of the tradition.

Another theory, advanced by Fergusson,[1] is that the temple was built in the reign of Jahangir. He says that " the temple as it now stands was commenced by some nameless Hindus, in honour of Siva, during the tolerant reign of Jahangir ; and that the building was stopped at the date engraved at the staircase, A.H. 1069 (A.D. 1659), the first year of the reign of the bigoted Aurangzeb. It was then unfinished, and has consequently remained a ruin ever since, which may give it an ancient look."[2] But Fergusson's conclusion was based on arguments which appear to have little foundation. Among other things the Jesuit Catrou, who published his *History of the Mughal Empire* in 1708 A.D., only one year after Aurangzeb's death, says that the Kashmiris are descended from the Jews. " *Moses* is a very common name there ; and some Ancient Monuments still to be seen discover 'em to be a People come out of *Israel*. For instance the *ruins* of an Edifice built on a high mountain is called at this Day the Throne of Solomon." Again, Bernier,[3] who accompanied Aurangzeb to Kashmir in 1665, writes of the existence of an " *extremely ancient building*, which bears evident marks of having been a temple for idols, although named Tact-Souliman, the Throne of Solomon." These statements show that as early as the beginning of the reign

---

[1] Fergusson, vol. i, p. 225. For a full discussion of the various theories on the subject see *infra*, p. 191 *et seq*.

[2] *Op. cit.*, p. 196.　　　　　　　　　[3] Bernier, p. 399.

of Aurangzeb the origin and authorship of the temple were lost in the mists of antiquity. They also prove that the temple had already fallen into disuse and ruin; and its construction, therefore, could not have been begun in the reign of Jahangir and stopped by Aurangzeb.

Kalhana, in his *Rajatarangini* (i, verse 341), definitely states that king Gopaditya built a shrine of Jyeshthesvara on the Gopadri (modern Takht-i-Sulaiman), but it cannot be asserted with certainty that the present temple is the same as that which was built by Gopaditya. It appears, however, probable that that shrine occupied the same position. Gopaditya's date, and consequently that of his buildings, is uncertain. But the conjecture that the present temple must be at least a century or so earlier than that highly finished example of Kashmir architecture, the Martand temple, seems plausible.

To the north of the base is a low cell 10′ 8″ square, entered through a plain and nearly circular-headed low doorway. The ceiling is flat and built of plain stone slabs placed on long stone joists, which rest on remarkably long beams supported on two octagonal columns.

To the south-east of the temple base, slightly lower down the hill, is a tank 10′ 1″ square.

In the area in front of the temple are the ruins of two Muslim structures, probably the remains of the small mosque and garden mentioned by Bernier, and belonging perhaps to the reign of Shah Jahan, when the Persian and Arabic inscriptions in the temple were put up.

The temple of Śankaracharya commands one of the finest views in the whole of Kashmir. The view of the city with its green, turfed roofs, covered in the spring with iris, tulip, and a variety of other flowers, is without a doubt unique.

KHANQAH OF SHAH HAMADAN

The city of Srinagar can best and most conveniently be seen from the river. The streets are narrow and often muddy. The river and the canals, on the other hand, form a very pleasant means of communication. As the visitor floats down the sluggish streams many objects attract his attention. The large and imposing palaces, the modern temples with tin-plated spires glittering in the sun, the brawny, loquacious boatmen plying their little airy craft, their pretty rosy-cheeked babies sprawling in the bottom, heedless of the shrill warnings of the distracted mothers, the curious cantilever bridges which span the river at short intervals—with these and the multifarious other objects of interest and amusement which usually appeal to the newcomer in Kashmir, the present monograph is not concerned. The attention of the reader is therefore specially invited to the extremely large number of architectural stones belonging to ancient Hindu temples which have now been built into the retaining walls of the river banks.

Between the third and fourth bridges on the right bank stands the Khanqah of Shah Hamadan, or, to give him his proper name, Mir Sayyid Ali Hamadani (Plate VI). Tradition ascribes his origin to the city of Hamadan in Persia. Legend further adds that Timur "was one night wandering in disguise about the streets of his capital, Samarkand, and overheard an old man and his wife talking over the prospects of starvation; upon which he took off an armlet, threw it to them, and departed unseen. A pretender Syud, or descendant of the prophet, asked them how they came by the armlet, and accused them of having stolen it. The matter was made known to Timur, who sagaciously decreed that the owner must be the person who could produce the fellow armlet. He then displayed it in his own possession, and ordered the accuser to undergo the ordeal of hot iron, which he refused, and was put to death in consequence. Timur, moreover, put to death all the other pretender Syuds in the country.

One, named Syud Ali or Shah Hamadan, who really was a descendant of the prophet, accused Timur of impiety, and told him that he would not remain in his country; and by virtue of his sanctity he was able to transport himself through the air to Kashmir.   He descended where the Masjid now stands, and told the Hindu fakir to depart. He refused, upon which Shah Hamadan said that if he would bring him news from heaven, he would then believe that he was a great man.   The fakir, who had the care of numerous images, immediately despatched one of them to heaven, upon which Shah Hamadan kicked his slipper after it with such force that the image fell to the ground.   He then asked the fakir how he became so great a man; he replied, by doing charitable actions; upon which Shah Hamadan thought him worthy of being made a convert to Islam; and in a few days so many more followed his example that two and a half kirwahs [*kharwār*=nearly two maunds] of Juneos, or sacred strings worn by the Brahmans, were delivered up by the Hindu proselytes.   The converted fakir himself was called Shyk Baba Wuli [Shaikh Baba Wali], and a penance of forty days performed at his shrine is considered the *ne plus ultra* of the meritorious."[1]   Whatever the religious value of this story, it is certain that the Sayyid must have been a personage of great importance, inasmuch as a number of shrines throughout the valley have been dedicated to his memory.

It is difficult to determine the date of the present structure, but it is practically certain that it does not belong to the time traditionally ascribed to the migration of Sayyid Ali Hamadani to Kashmir. Baron von Hügel, who visited Kashmir in 1835, speaks of it as a modern-looking building.   But there is no doubt that a mosque or some such religious edifice stood here at least as early as the reign of Akbar; for Abul Fazl in his *Ain-i-Akbari* says that " Mir Sayyid Ali Hamadani resided for some time in this city (Srinagar), and a monastery founded by him still preserves his name."

Apart from the cloisters, which have been added later, and the

[1] Vigne, vol. ii, pp. 82-83.

additions and alterations that are being carried on by its present-day caretakers, the original building is a square structure. Its chief structural peculiarity is that it is for the most part built of wooden balks. The spaces between the balks are filled by very small and carefully dressed bricks. Some of the doors and windows are beautiful examples of wood carving, and the wooden cornice of the plinth is an exquisite piece of workmanship.

The interior consists of a single large hall 63′ by 43′. On the southern and northern sides are fourteen chambers which now serve the purpose of godowns. The one in the north-west corner contains the tomb of the saint. The only decoration in the interior is the very beautiful panelled wood-work on the walls, to which age has imparted a rich brown colour. The dado consists of a number of panels decorated with carved floral patterns. The larger panels in the walls bear carved on them the names of God, which have been painted in gold. A strong contrast with the sombre hue of the walls is furnished by the glass and glazed work which decorates the external surface of the chamber containing the mausoleum.

The ceiling is supported in the centre on four wooden columns, covered with pieces of wood arranged in fish-bone patterns which originally bore painted inscriptions. Their bases have been carved with lotus leaves, and their capitals, which are sixteen-sided, are adorned with acanthus (?) leaf decoration.

Two ladders at the sides give access to the balconies above. The upper floor does not possess any points of interest.

Over the doorway of the shrine is carved an inscription which gives 786 Hijra as the year of Shah Hamadan's death. This date corresponds to A.D. 1384.

Patthar Masjid

" Of the Mughal style as exemplified by buildings in Kashmir it is not necessary to say much, because the style is practically the same as that at Agra, Delhi, and Lahore. The only differences which suggest themselves are that a local grey limestone was generally used in Kashmir for face work; and white marble, owing no doubt to the difficulties of transport, is hardly ever seen."[1]   This stone is an excellent material for mouldings and for carving, and is capable of receiving a very high polish, as is testified by the pillars in the pavilion at Shalimar.   Of the Mughal mosques in Kashmir, the Patthar Masjid, "The Stone Mosque," so called in contradistinction to the indigenous wooden mosques of the valley, is the largest surviving example (Plate VII).   The façade consists of nine arches, including the large arched portico in the centre.   The arched openings are enclosed in shallow decorative cusped arches, which in their turn are enclosed in rectangular frames.   The *horizontal* construction of these arches is remarkable.   All of them have recently been closed up with rubble stone masonry.

The half-attached " bedpost " columns in the two outer angles of the jambs of the entrance are noteworthy.   The plinth, which is now mostly underground, is surmounted by a lotus-leaf coping.

The frieze between the projecting cornice and the eaves is decorated with a series of large lotus leaves, carved in relief, some of which have been pierced, and thus made to serve the purpose of ventilation apertures.   A flight of steps in each jamb of the entrance gives access to the roof, which is, as usual in Kashmir, sloping, except in the centre, where there was originally a dome which was later dismantled by the Sikhs.   The roof consists of twenty-seven domes, the central one of which is the largest.   The domes are mostly ribbed inside, though there are some which are flat or waggon-vaulted.

The roof is supported internally on eighteen extraordinarily massive square columns having projections on two sides.   The lower portion of the columns is built of stone and the upper of brick covered by a thick coat of buff-coloured lime plaster.

The enclosure wall is built of brick masonry, with a coat of lime plaster, adorned by a range of shallow arched niches.

[1] *A.S.R.*, 1906-7, p. 169.

The mosque is said to have been built in A.D. 1623 by the Empress Nur Jahan. There is a tradition that, being once questioned regarding the cost of its construction, she pointed to her jewelled slippers and replied, "As much as that." The jest was reported to the mullahs, who unanimously decreed that by this sacrilegious allusion the mosque had become desecrated, and was unfit for religious use. For this reason the Patthar Masjid has never been used as a place of prayer.

TOMB OF ZAIN-UL-ABIDIN'S MOTHER

A couple of furlongs lower down the river, between the fourth and the fifth bridges, is the Sri Ranbir Ganj, the busiest and most important trading mart in Kashmir. Near it are seen the high and massive domes of the tomb of the mother of Zain-ul-abidin, towering far above the gabled roofs of the surrounding houses (Plate VIII).

The most attractive chapter in the history of the Muslim rule in Kashmir is the reign of Zain-ul-abidin (1421-1472). He was a patron of the arts and industries, and as tolerant to his Hindu subjects as his father, Sikandar But-shikan, was bigoted. But though he is said to have occasionally made pilgrimages to Hindu shrines, he does not seem to have scrupled in using Hindu remains for his own purposes. The superstructure alone of his mother's tomb was erected by him. The plinth with its filleted torus cornice is entirely Hindu (Plate LXXIV); so is the trefoiled entrance and its still undisturbed massive jambs. In plan it is square, with the angles cut off and replaced by rectangular projections. The superstructure follows the same plan, and consists of a single chamber in the middle with projections recessed internally at the angles, roofed over by five domes, the largest naturally being in the centre.

"Its principal features are the glazed and moulded blue bricks, which are studded at intervals in the exterior walls, the semicircular brick projections, on the drum of the main dome, and the moulded string-courses and sunk panels on the drums of the cupolas."[1]

[1] *A.S.R.*, 1906-7, p. 162.

6

The wooden lintels of the ventilation apertures are remarkably well preserved.

Inside, hanging from an iron plate attached to the apex of the central dome, is an iron chain which has given rise to the misconception, common among the Hindus of Kashmir, that the structure in its present shape was originally a Panchamukha (five-faced or five-headed) temple, such chains being usually found in Hindu shrines, attached to the principal bell.

Immediately to the north of this building is a Hindu enclosure wall with gateway, which contains a number of tombs, one of which is said to preserve the remains of the king himself. This wall, like that of the Śankaracharya temple, has been the object of much controversy. Cunningham and Cole ascribed it to a date as early as the fourth or fifth century A.D. This theory was contested by Fergusson, who, on the strength of the resemblance of the miniature arches which decorate this wall to similar decorative features in Muslim architecture, maintained that it was built by the Muslims themselves at the time they erected the mausoleum. But it is probable that Cunningham and Cole, who actually saw it, were nearer the truth than Fergusson, who judged only from photographs. The wall is a real Hindu one, as its materials and massiveness amply prove, though it is undoubtedly later than the fifth century A.D. A further proof of its Hindu origin is the number of carved stones still found round the site, which bear sculptured reliefs of Hindu deities.

The whole group is enclosed in a massive stone wall with a ridged coping.

This outer wall, as well as its two entrances, one on the riverside and the other opening on the road, likewise date back to Hindu times.

Since the time of Zain-ul-abidin this enclosure has been used as a cemetery, and many of the notabilities of Muslim Kashmir are interred here, among them the famous Tartar invader Mirza Haidar Gurgan, the cousin of Babar, who made his first raid into Kashmir

from Turkistan and occupied it a second time in the name of
Humayun, during the latter's exile from Hindustan. The following in-
scription on his tombstone gives the date of his death (A.H. 958 =
A.D. 1551).

> Shah Gurgan Mirza Haidar akhir
> Ba mulke shahadat zadah kus-i shahi
> Qaza-e Ilahi chunin bud-o tarikh
> Shuda bahr-i vaslash, Qaza-e Ilahi.

Translation : " At last the King Mirza Haidar Gurgan beat his royal drum (to an-
nounce his departure) for the realm of martyrdom.   Such was the will of God and (even)
the date of his union (with God) is contained in (the phrase) ' will of God.' "

Pir Haji Muhammad Sahib

Less than half a mile from the ruins described above, on the way
to the Jama' Masjid by way of Safa Kadal, is another enclosure with a
structure in the centre, which is now doing duty as the tomb of Pir
Haji Muhammad, a Muslim saint.   In plan it is similar to the tomb
of Zain-ul-abidin's mother, the only difference being that this has
two flights of steps facing east and west, and the latter has only one,
which faces west.   There is no doubt that the plinth and the corners
of the superstructure, as they are at present, are in their original
position, and have never been tampered with.

The spaces between the stone pilasters at the corners have been
filled in with screen walls of *kanjur* masonry, the larger sides of which
are decorated externally with three closed panels.   This appears to
have been a later addition.   A curious fact about this structure is that
the two flights of steps are also later additions, though undoubtedly
they have been transplanted from some Hindu site.   Proof for this
conjecture is furnished by the fact that the cornice of the plinth, a
cyma recta, is not bonded with the masonry of the stairs, and that
carved stones evidently not originally intended for the purpose have
been used in the steps.

In the eastern corner of the courtyard is a smaller enclosure partitioned off from the main area; this also contains a trefoiled niche and some fluted columns.

There is a small square Muslim brick tomb within the compound wall.

The position of these ruins suggested to Sir Aurel Stein their " possible identity with the temple of Vishnu Ranasvamin which Kalhana mentions as founded by King Ranaditya. This temple must have enjoyed considerable celebrity up to a comparatively late period."[1]

JAMA‘ MASJID

The history of the Jama‘ Masjid of Srinagar is a singularly chequered one. Its original conception and erection are ascribed to Sikandar But-shikan, who reigned in Kashmir from A.D. 1390-91 to 1414-15. He is said to have laid its foundation in A.D. 1398 and completed it in 1402. His illustrious son Zain-ul-abidin is reported to have greatly exerted himself in adding to its æsthetic attractions. He also established an Islamic school as an appendage to the mosque, and endowed it with estates to enable it to defray the cost of maintenance. In A.D. 1479 a large conflagration reduced it to ashes, and the then reigning sovereign, Sultan Hasan Shah, set about its reconstruction with greater splendour. Unfortunately the king died before completing his task, which was brought to a successful end in A.D. 1503 by Ibrahim Magre, Commander-in-Chief of the Kashmir forces, in the reigns of Muhammad Shah and Fateh Shah. In the year 1620, in the reign of Jahangir, a severe conflagration again broke out in Srinagar and destroyed twelve thousand buildings, among them the Jama‘ Masjid. The emperor, who is stated to have been in Kashmir at the time, immediately directed its reconstruction, which was taken in hand and completed in the space of seventeen years. Malik Haidar of Tsodur, the historian of Kashmir, was entrusted with the execution of the work. The inscription on the southern entrance, which was erected about this time, gives the history of the mosque up to this date.

[1] *Rajat.*, vol. ii, p. 447.

In addition to restoration of the mosque the emperor bestowed munificent grants of land, not only for its upkeep, but also to provide subsistence allowance for the caretakers.   I'taqad Khan, a provincial governor of Kashmir during the reign of Shah Jahan, was a gross tyrant.   The emperor on a visit to Kashmir dismissed him, and appointed Zafar Khan, the son of the Prime Minister, Asaf Khan, as his successor.   The latter drew up a list of the irregularities practised in Kashmir by his predecessor, and submitted it to the emperor, who in a royal *farmān*, or decree, directed remission of all the petty exactions which the former local governors had inflicted upon the inhabitants of the valley.   The royal *farmān* was engraved on a block of black marble and set up on the right wall of the southern gateway of the Jama' Masjid, for the benefit of the public.   The document is of extraordinary interest, not only because it illustrates the ways and means to which some unscrupulous governors, gifted with more ingenuity than conscience, had recourse in their haste to amass a fortune, but also as an honourable testimony to the emperor's solicitude for the welfare of his distant Himalayan dependency.

In A.D. 1674 the mosque was for the third time destroyed by fire. It is stated that when the emperor Aurangzeb heard of the accident, his first enquiry was whether the chinars were safe; for he said " the mosque could be rebuilt in a short time; a full-grown chinar can never be quickly replaced."   He impressed all the bricklayers and masons of the city into his service, and had the mosque completed within the short period of three years.   In his restoration it is evident, both from the building itself and on the authority of history, that the Mughal strictly adhered to the plan of the original mosque of Sikandar Butshikan.   Aurangzeb seems to have spent a considerable sum of money on gilding and other evanescent embellishment of the mosque.

From the time of Aurangzeb down to 1914 the structural history of the mosque is a record of steady decay.   The fitful repairs by the Afghan governors did not arrest its downward progress to ruin.   In the earlier part of the Sikh régime in Kashmir the mosque was closed and its doors were blocked up.   After a period of twenty-one years, it was reopened by Ghulam Muhi-ud-din, the Sikh Governor, who spent nearly a lakh and a half of rupees on its repair.   In Dogra times attempts were more than once made to put it into repair, but they do not seem to have led to any appreciable result.   Since the year 1913, however, the Muslims of Kashmir, substantially aided by a grant from His Highness's Government, have put forth their best energies for the achievement of the difficult task, and it has recently been brought to a successful conclusion.

The mosque is a quadrangle and roughly square in plan, its northern and southern sides being 384' in length.   Its principal features are the four minars, one in the middle of each side (Plate IX). They are covered by a series of pyramidal roofs, which terminate in an open turret crowned by a high pinnacle (Plate X).   All these minars, except that to the west, which contains the pulpit, cover spacious arched entrances which are plain but very imposing.   The southern entrance seems, as now, to have always been the one most commonly used.   This is borne out by the fact that the inscriptions—among them Shah Jahan's *farmān*, which would naturally be placed at the most frequented spot in the mosque—have been built into the wall of this entrance.   The roof of each minar was supported on eight wooden columns, 50' in height and over 6' in girth, whose modern substitutes still stand on the original square limestone bases. The columns are plain and unornamented.   The minars are connected by spacious halls, the principal feature of which is the vast array of 378 wooden columns which support the roof.

The western minar differs from its companions of the other three sides in having slightly larger dimensions and two stairs, one in each jamb of the arch, giving access to the roof and each surmounted by a small brick dome.   The *gachh* (gypsum) plaster is inartistic and of recent date.

The compound is bisected by two broad paths, planned after the manner of a formal Mughal garden. At the point of their inter-section has been built a small and insignificant *bārahdarī*.

Formerly a small canal which entered through the eastern entrance used to feed the large, but now dilapidated, tank in the compound. The canal fell into disuse when the Srinagar water-works system was instituted. Its place is now taken by an ordinary P.W.D. water-supply. The water from the tank flows down a small ornamental stone chute, and passing out of the channel leaves the mosque by an underground passage in the west wall. After a meandering course of a quarter of a mile the pretty little rill, now replaced by the usual gutters, emptied itself into the Mar canal. The streamlet was in existence as recently as thirty years ago, and bore the name of Lachhma-kul. It was originally brought from the Sindh by King Zain-ul-abidin, and its first name was Zaina-Ganga.

The most charming feature of the compound, apart from the singularly imposing aspect of the arcaded front of the halls, is a group of shady chinars, which tradition assigns variously to Zain-ul-abidin's and Hasan Shah's reigns. But there seems to be little doubt that some, if not all of them, are of more recent growth.

The Hari Parbat Fort

The hill of Hari Parbat (Plate XI), crowned by the Pathan fort which is visible from every part of the city, has from time immemorial been a place of great sanctity in Kashmir. The name is the Kashmiri equivalent of the Sanskrit *śarika-parvata*, " the hill of Śarika " (har = Indian maina). Legend, corroborated by modern science, informs us that the valley was, in prehistoric times, a vast lake, which must have been one of the most beautiful in the world. In this lake dwelt the water-demon Jalodbhava. The Śarikamahatmya tells us, cir-cumstantially, the story of the defeat and destruction of this demon: how the monster wrought havoc among the mountains of the adjacent districts, but being invulnerable in his own element, and declining to fight at a disadvantage on land, continued his life of depredation in impudent security for a long time; how the gods fumed and stormed in impotent rage, and finally resolved to lay the matter before the Almighty Mother Sati, the controller of the titanic forces of nature; how she assumed the form of a Śarika bird (maina) and taking a pebble in her beak dropped it at the spot where she knew the demon was lying, lulled into false security; and finally how the pebble swelled into gigantic proportions and crushed the demon by its weight.   The pebble to this day survives under the name of Hari Parbat, and a depression in the ground outside the Sangin Darwaza of the fort wall is pointed out as the spot wherefrom the panting breath of the demon forced its way out, as he was struggling under the crushing weight over him.   The legend adds that the gods in grateful memory of their deliverance took up their abode here, which accounts for the fact that every individual stone, large and small, on this hill is reverenced by the orthodox Brahmans as the representative of one of the thirty-three crores of gods which comprise the Hindu pantheon.

In modern times, both Hindus and Muslims have appropriated parts of the hill for their shrines; but neither the shrine of Chakreśvari nor the ziarat of Makhdum Sahib possesses any architectural interest. The fort which crowns the summit is a commonplace structure (Plate XI), but this cannot be said of Akbar's rampart and its gates, Kathi Darwaza and Sangin Darwaza, and the mosque of Akhun Mulla Shah, which are well worth a visit.   The rampart, which is for the most part in ruins, is nearly 3 miles in circumference. The Kathi Darwaza seems to have been the principal entrance, judging from the fact that the inscriptions have been put up only here.   It is a very simple structure, comprising a domed chamber in the middle with two side-recesses.   Its only external decorations are rectangular and arched panels and two beautiful medallions, in high relief, on the spandrels of the arch.

Akbar's inscription runs as follows:—

Bina-e qila'-e Nagar-Nagar bud
Ba 'ahad-e padshah-e dad-gustar
Sar-e Shahan-i 'alam Shah Akbar
T'ali Shanahu Allah-u Akbar
Shahanshah-e ki dar 'alam misalash
Na bud ast-o na khwahad bud digar
Karor-o dah lakh az makhzan firistad
Du sad ustad Hindi jumla chakar
Na kardah hechkas bigar anja
Tamami yaftand az makhzanash zar
Chil-o char az julusi padshahi
Hazar-o shash zi tarikh-e payambar.

Translation : The foundation of the fort of Nagar-Nagar was laid in the reign of the just sovereign, the king of kings, Akbar, unparalleled among the kings of the world, past or future. He sent one crore and ten lakhs (of rupees) from his treasury and two hundred Indian master-builders, all his servants. No one was forced to work without remuneration. All obtained their wages from his treasury. (In the) forty-fourth year after the accession of the Emperor (and) 1006 after the prophet.

The second inscription was erected by the officer in charge of the works and runs as follows:—

Bina-e qila'-e Nagar-Nagar ba-'aun Allah
Ba hukm-i Shah-i Jahan Zilallah Akbar Shah
Ba sa'ye Mir Muhammad Husain gasht tamam
Haqir banda-e az banda-ha-e Akbar Shah
Dawam-i daulat-i in Shah ta abad bada
Ba haqq-i Shahidan La-ilaha-il-allah.

Translation : The foundation of the fort of Nagar Nagar was completed, by favour of the Almighty, under orders of the king of the world, Shadow of God, Emperor Akbar, and through the instrumentality of Mir Muhammad Hussain, the least among the servants of King Akbar. May the prosperity of this king endure for ever, through the grace of the martyrs of the Faith. There is no God but God.

The Sangin Darwaza, " the stone gate," differs from Kathi Darwaza in being more ornate. The exterior is decorated by two corbelled windows, and there are two stairs, one on each side, which give access to the roof.

According to tradition, which is still living, the construction of the Hari Parbat, or, as Akbar named it, Nagar-Nagar, rampart was started as a relief work, to alleviate the distress of the people during a famine. The historian Śuka states that the emperor, on hearing of the hardship inflicted upon the citizens by the troops, who for want of accommodation had been quartered upon them, had a cantonment built on the slopes of the Hari Parbat hill, which from that time became a flourishing settlement. Bernier, who saw it three-quarters of a century later, speaks of it as " an isolated hill, with handsome houses on its declivity, each having a garden."

AKHUN MULLA SHAH'S MOSQUE

The little mosque situated a little way up the hill below the shrine of Makhdum Sahib was built by the crown prince Dara Shikoh, son of Shah Jahan, for his tutor Akhun Mulla Shah (Plate XII). It is built of a beautiful grey limestone. The stone lotus finial over the pulpit is the only example of its kind surviving in Kashmir. The only external decorations are the rectangular panels enclosing cusped arches. " Its plan is singular, the design of the prayer chamber being repeated on the east side of the courtyard and forming the gateway. On the north and the south sides of the courtyard are arcades, treated in the same way as the wings of the prayer chamber. Usually the arcades round the quadrangle in front of a mosque are treated quite differently from any part of the prayer chamber. The somewhat cramped proportions of the courtyard in this case may be due to the slope of the hill on which it stands, and the difficulty which would have been experienced in making the prayer chamber wider."[1]

On a lower level are the ruins of the arched halls wherein pilgrims used to lodge. A little further off is the hammam,

[1] *A.S.R.*, 1906-7, pp. 169-170.

which is now closed up. On the lintel of its doorway is the following inscription:—

> Tarikh-i hammam-o masjid-i Sultan Dara Shikoh
> Hammam-i tu o masjidat ai dida baz
> Garm ast yake yake jama'at pardaz
> Tarikh-i bina-i har du ra goyad Shah
> Yak ja-i wazu amad-o yak ja-i namaz.

Translation : The date of the construction of the hammam and the mosque of Sultan Dara Shikoh.

Thy hammam and thy mosque : one affords warmth and the other adorns the congregation. The king tells the date of the foundation of both : the one is the place of ablution and the other the place of worship.

The last line contains the chronogram giving the date, A.H. 1059, corresponding to A.D. 1649.

CEMETERY OF BAHA-UD-DIN

Outside the rampart at a distance of less than two furlongs from the mosque of Akhun Mulla Shah is the cemetery of Baha-ud-din Sahib. It contains numerous Hindu remains, among them the ruins of a massive gateway standing near the entrance, which is traditionally believed to be a part of the "Pravareśa" temple built by Pravaresena II. It also contains the graves of some of the most prominent personages of Muslim Kashmir. One of the tombstones bears a bilingual Sanskrit and Arabic inscription which mentions the name of Muhammad Shah, the puppet ruler who was made king and dethroned no less than four times.

MOSQUE AND TOMB OF MADIN SAHIB

Among the pre-Mughal Muslim buildings of Kashmir, one of the most prominent is the mosque of Madin Sahib at Zadibal. It is also interesting as it shows to perfection the way in which the early Muslims used the materials of the Hindu temples. The group of buildings at Vitsarnag and a number of others strewn about the city belong to this series.

The base is square and is built entirely of materials belonging to a plinth of a mediæval temple. Even the arrangement of courses is identical with that of the ordinary temple base. The superstructure consists of four walls, adorned externally with trefoiled brick niches. The upper foil is pointed, but in the case of the doorway it is ogee-shaped. The corner pilasters of the walls as well as pilasters of the niches stand upon bases, and are surmounted by capitals which are purely Hindu in style. The spandrels of the arches of the niches are decorated with beautiful tracery work. Their entablature is distinctly Hindu. The cornice over the walls is composed of half a dozen courses of wood, the most prominent feature of which is the double series of dentils and metopes, the latter bearing delicate open-work carving. Above these are the eaves, which are adorned with a row of wooden tongues projecting downwards. The chamber is covered by a pyramidal earth and birch-bark roof overgrown with a jungle of white and blue irises. On the apex of the pyramid was the spire, the only remnants of which that exist are a single long upright pole and a few pieces of timber. The entrance to the mosque is, of course, through the east wall. The wooden doorway is elaborately carved, and is flanked by two fluted stone columns originally belonging to the adjoining Hindu ruins. The interior is plain. The ceiling of *khatamband* (thin pieces of wood worked into geometrical patterns) is supported on four multi-sided wooden columns.

To the north of the mosque is the tomb of the saint. In ancient times it must have presented a brilliant spectacle, as its entire wall surface was decorated with glazed tiles, most of which have unfortunately been removed and sold out of Kashmir. A few fragments are preserved in the Pratap Singh Museum, Srinagar. When Nicholls of the Archæological Survey of India visited Kashmir in 1905, he found considerable portions of the tile decoration in good preservation. The left spandrel of the entrance arch was adorned with a very well executed representation of a beast with the body of a leopard, changing at the neck into the trunk of a human being, shooting apparently with a bow and arrow at its own tail, while a

fox is quietly looking on among flowers and " cloud-forms." The
" cloud-forms " are common in Chinese and Persian art. The
principal beast in the picture is about 4 feet long, and strikes quite
an heraldic attitude. The human chest, shoulders, and head are unfortunately missing. The tail ends in a kind of dragon's head. As
for the colours, the background is blue, the trunk of the man is red,
the leopard's body is yellow with light green spots, the dragon's head
and the fox are reddish-brown, the flowers are of various colours.
Besides the spandrels there is more tile-work in the building. The
jambs of the archway are lined with squares, many of which have
fallen out and been put back in the wrong place. None of these
is of any special interest, except that they show that tile-work was
used on masonry buildings in Kashmir before Mughal days. There
is, however, an interesting narrow border above the dado on the east
façade representing a flowing floral pattern interwoven with the heads
of donkeys and lions.

Both the tomb and the mosque were built in memory of the
same person, and the inscription on the lintel of the entrance of
the mosque records the date of its erection as A.H. 888 (A.D. 1483) in
the reign of Zain-ul-abidin. The tomb may have been built a few
years later, though it is not impossible that it was built at the same
time as the mosque, for among Muslims the practice of building
tombs during the lifetime of their future occupants is not uncommon.

Around these two structures, and on the way between them and
the Sangin Darwaza of the fort, there are numerous Hindu remains,
all of which have grievously suffered at the hands of the iconoclast.
Many of them have been converted into mosques, though even these
latter have now fallen into desuetude.

MUGHAL GARDENS

The valley of Kashmir provided a magnificent field for the
garden-planning genius of the Imperial Mughals. Its salubrity of
climate, its inexhaustible supply of water, its grassy alluvial mountain

slopes, presented opportunities which the emperors certainly did not neglect. Some of the most charming spots in a valley which itself has deservedly obtained the title of the " Paradise of the Indies " were selected as royal pleasure haunts; and during the four successive reigns of the greatest of the Mughal emperors a series of splendid gardens was constructed, which are famous in the world for their natural charm and beauty of environment. Among the gardens on the banks of the Dal, Chashma-i-Shahi, Nishat, and Shalimar are the best preserved and most frequented. Remains of other gardens exist, but they are far too ruinous to merit the attention of the modern visitor; among these perhaps the most notable was the Bagh-i-Nagin, the garden of Akbar. Nasim, situated opposite to the Shalimar Bagh, contains a splendid park of shady old chinars.

CHASHMA-I-SHAHI

This is the smallest, though not on that account the least attractive, of the Mughal gardens of Kashmir. It is situated at a distance of five and a half miles from Srinagar, a little less than a mile off the road to Nishat. The conformation of the ground round about shows that the garden can never have been large, but there is evidence to prove that it was not as circumscribed as it is now. The two *bārahdarīs* as well as the surrounding wall and the side entrance belong to recent times. The cascades, the plinths of the *barahdaris*, the water-courses, tanks, and fountains, are genuine Mughal works, save, of course, for the restorations. The lowest terrace has a tank in the centre containing five fountains arranged as a quincunx. A flight of steps on each side of the *barahdari* leads up to the second terrace and to the ground-floor of the *barahdari* itself. This is one of the most favoured haunts of tourists in spring and early summer, for the view it commands of the Dal lake is one of the most charming that can be had anywhere, at any rate among those which are easy of access. In spring, when the fields of the blossoming rape-seed flank the verdant hill slopes with gold; when the snow-capped mountains are being ceaselessly washed by melting snows and frequent showers; when in sunny intervals white masses of downy clouds are seen floating majestically in the translucent azure of the sky, their shadows trailing after them as if caught by the sharp mountain peaks; when the lake is free from weeds and reeds—beardless, as the Kashmiris call it—and its two small islets of Rupalank and Sonalank, the Chahar-chinar, are like two emeralds set in the sapphire shield of the Dal; when vast patches of the slopes of the Chashma-i-Shahi hill and the Hari Parbat are covered with red and white almond blossoms, the fortunate spectator stands entranced as he gazes out of the arch of the *barahdari*, his feelings lulled by the gentle murmur of the little fountain that plays in the centre of the hall.

The tank in the second terrace contains only one fountain and a small carved chute, down which the water of the channels in the upper terraces comes rippling joyously. All these fountains, channels, and cascades are fed by the real Chashma-i-Shahi, a truly "royal" spring, which perennially gives forth its wealth of the coolest and purest water in a lotus basin built in the centre of a Mughal platform. The pavilion which covers it is unusually ugly and dilapidated. According to an inscription said to have been put up at the gateway, the garden was constructed in the reign of Shah Jahan, probably by the emperor himself. The exact wording of the verse which contained the date is as follows:

> Guftamash bahr-i Chashma tarikhe,
> Guft bar go kausar-i Shahi.

Translation : " I enquired of him regarding the date of the spring; he replied, ' say kausar-i shahi ' (the royal spring)."

The term *kausar-i-shāhī* is synonymous with Chashma-i-Shahi, and according to the abjad system of reckoning gives the Hijra year 1042, corresponding with A.D. 1632-33.

Pari Mahal

The striking group of arched terraces perched higher up on the mountain slope to the west of Chashma-i-Shahi is Pari Mahal, "the fairies' abode," a ruined garden palace, the construction of which is ascribed by tradition to the ill-starred prince Dara Shikoh, who was beheaded in 1659 by order of his brother Aurangzeb. Despite its dilapidated condition, it is easy to determine its principal features; for the garden has, probably owing to its difficulty of access, escaped the restoration to which the other Mughal gardens in Kashmir have been subjected. Pari Mahal differs from other Kashmir gardens in that it does not possess any cascades or water chutes, though it seems probable that there were fountains in the tanks. Water was mainly conducted by underground earthen pipes, though a few traces of open water-courses have also been found. The garden consists of six terraces, with a total length of about 400'. The width of the terraces varies from 179' to 205'.

In the uppermost terrace are the ruins of two structures, a *barahdari* facing the lake, and a water reservoir built against the mountainside. The reservoir was fed from above by a spring, which has since gone dry, and of which the only extant remains are the fragmentary stone conduit and the retaining wall against the hill-side. It is a simple chamber, built of rubble stones in lime, with a façade of two small arches. Internally it measures 11' 3" by 5', and has a recess in each of its walls. Water flowed through an arched drain pierced in the front wall which is now partially blocked up. At each corner of the terrace wall is a flight of steps leading to the lower terrace, measuring 22' 3" by 4' 3".

In the middle of the second terrace exactly in front of the *barahdari* is a large tank with brick sides measuring 39' 6" by 26' 6". The façade of the retaining wall is ornamented with a series of twenty-one arches, including two of the side-stairs. The arches are built in descending order of height from the centre. Each of them is surmounted by a niche, the height of which increases in proportion to decrease in the height of the arch. The central arch is covered with a coat of fine painted plaster, which seems to have always served as a favourite board for scribbling notices in pen and pencil. Various people have recorded on this the date of their visit to the garden. Among them was the cruel Azad Khan, a Pathan Governor. His amanuensis, Malik Sabir Munshi, has scribbled the following sentence in black ink:

" Batarikhi bist-o nuhum mahi Rabi-us-sani s. 1199. . . . Ittifaq bahamrahi sawari kasir-ul-iqtidar Sardar Azad Khan nazim-i sūba-i Kashmir mutabiq sair-o shikar warid-i in makan farhat asar gardidah " Faqir haqir Malik Sabir Munshi.

Translation : " On the 29th of Rabi-us-sani s. 1199 (A.D. 1784-85) the humble mendicant Malik Sabir Munshi visited this abode of bliss in the suite of the most honourable Sardar Azad Khan, Governor of the Province of Kashmir, while (he was) on an expedition for pleasure and sport."

This terrace seems to have been screened off from the lower court by a parapet wall, which is still extant in parts.

The third terrace is, architecturally, the most interesting portion of the garden. The entrance, which is of the usual Mughal type, arched in front and behind with a central domed chamber, is in the middle of the east wall, and is covered with a coat of fine painted plaster. On either side of it are a series of spacious rooms: the one to its north seems to have been the hammam. Fragments of the water-pipe are still to be seen projecting from a corner of its domed ceiling. Its interior is the most highly decorated of all the rooms in Pari Mahal. On the south side of the entrance are two other chambers, but it is difficult to say to what use they were put. Both of them have pipes inserted into their ceilings, the one nearest the gateway having only one, but the other, two; possibly the latter chamber was used as a kitchen. The western half of the retaining wall has recently fallen; doubtless it also contained chambers similar to those on the other side.

In the central recess of the arcade is visible the originally hidden

7

earthen pipe which conveyed water from the terrace above. From it the water flowed through an open channel and an underground pipe, which ran side by side, and entered the *barahdari* at the middle of the broad end of the terrace. In all probability the channel formed a tank in the centre of the principal chamber and then emptied itself into the pipe which ran underground, of which traces are still visible on the floor of the *barahdari*.

It is probable that these three terraces were reserved solely for the prince's private use.

The fourth terrace has nothing remarkable in it except the ruins of the tank—perhaps it was a tank within a *barahdari*—whose plinth projects far beyond the line of the wall. About the middle of its north wall is the earthen pipe which conducted water to the terrace below.

In the fifth terrace a curious feature of the plinth of the *barahdari*, or the tank, of the upper terrace is the numerous square holes with which the upper half of its surface is perforated. They were probably intended to harbour flocks of pigeons. The retaining wall is arcaded. The arcade is a double one, the upper row of arches faced a corridor which ran on both sides of the plinth of the *barahdari*.

The sixth and the last terrace has a rectangular tank in the middle and octagonal bastions at the ends. The lower end is not supported by any retaining wall.

The ruined structure a few yards below seems to have been intended for a kind of a guard house.

NISHAT BAGH

Returning from the Chashma-i-Shahi to the main road, the visitor proceeds 2½ miles to Nishat Bagh. This is the most favoured resort of pleasure-seekers in Kashmir. "Its twelve terraces, one for each sign of the zodiac, rise dramatically high and higher up the mountain-side from the eastern shore of the lake. The stream tears foaming down the carved cascades, and fountains play in every tank and water-course, filling the garden with their joyous life and movement. The flower beds on these sunny terraces blaze with colour—roses, lilies, geraniums, asters, gorgeous tall-growing zinnias, and feathery cosmos, pink and white. Beautiful at all times, when autumn lights up the poplars in clear gold and the big chenars burn red against the dark blue rocky background, there are few more brilliant, more breathlessly entrancing sights than this first view of Asaf Khan's Garden of Gladness "[1] (Plate XIII).

The lowest terrace has unfortunately been cut off by the modern road, which has likewise shorn Shalimar of part of its length. The two wooden doorways as well as the gaudily painted *barahdari* on the third terrace are innovations which date from the time of Wazir Pannu's governorship of Kashmir in the reign of the late Maharaja Ranbir Singhji. These Mughal gardens of Kashmir owe a heavy debt of gratitude to this gentleman, if not for restoring them to their original grandeur, at any rate for arresting their further decay. He also repaired them thoroughly according to his lights; and if his *barahdaris* and porticoes do not bear comparison with similar structures of the Mughals, not he but the times to which he belonged are responsible.

The brightest and most fragrant spot in the garden is undoubtedly the second terrace, with its thick groves of Persian lilacs, its high, broad, and vertical cascade of sparkling water, and its beds of brilliant pansies. The twenty-three small niches in the arched recess immediately behind the cascade were originally intended to contain rows of lamps, whose flickering light, reflected and multiplied in the transparent sheet of water behind which they lay, must have presented a singularly pleasing spectacle at night.

Two flights of stone steps which survive from the date of their original construction give access to the third terrace. The *barahdari* is a two-storied structure. In the middle of the lower floor " is a

[1] Mrs. Villiers-Stuart, *Gardens of the Great Mughals*, p. 168.

reservoir about fourteen feet square and three feet deep, with five fountains, the one in the centre being the only old stone fountain left in the garden.   On a summer day there are few more attractive rooms than the fountain hall of this Kashmir garden house.   The gay colours of the carved woodwork shine through the spray in delightful contrast with the dull green running water.   Through a latticed arch a glimpse is caught of the brilliant garden terraces and their waterfalls flashing white against the mountain-side.   Looking over the lake which glitters below in the sunshine, the views of the valley are bounded by the distant snow-capped peaks, the far country of the Pir Panjal. Climbing roses twine about the painted wooden pillars, and nod their creamy flowers through the openings of the lattice.   All the long afternoon a little breeze ruffles the surface of the lake and blows in the scent of the flowers, mingling it with the drifting fountain spray; for the terrace below the pavilion is planted after the old custom with a thicket of Persian lilac."[1]

Here begins the long series of open terraces—each rising higher than the one preceding it—which terminates in the eleventh terrace at the upper end of the garden. They are bisected by a broad water-course, which on certain days in the week is converted into a bounteous stream with numerous fountains playing in its midst, saturating the atmosphere with their driving spray.   A feature of this garden are the beautiful marble thrones which span the water-courses at intervals. These are now, as they undoubtedly were in Mughal times, the favourite seats of visitors to the garden.   The tank in the eleventh terrace contains a group of twenty-five fountains.   From this terrace a flight of stone steps leads to the last, and, in the eyes of its Mughal founder, Asaf Khan, the most sacred part of the garden, the zenana enclosure.   The low parapet wall which screened this terrace from the remainder of the garden is still in existence.   At the upper end of the footpath near the pavilion is a remnant of the original brick pavement.   An octagonal tower is built at each end of the retaining

[1] Mrs. Villiers-Stuart, *Gardens of the Great Mughals*, pp. 173-74.

wall of the terrace, and contains a stair which leads down to the lower and more exposed parts of the garden.

Strolling down the flower-bordered walks on the right side of the channel, the visitor who makes his exit into the second terrace will notice two rather well-executed elephants, standing on either side of a vase containing lotuses, carved on the stone lintel of the doorway. The presence of these animals would show, if other evidence were wanting, which is not the case, that the Nishat Bagh was built before the time of Aurangzeb. Perhaps he did not enter the garden, as it was a private one, and did not belong to the king, which may also account for Bernier not mentioning it.

The original approach to the garden was from the lake, which was also its lower boundary. The old flight of stone steps which gave direct access to the garden is still in an excellent state of preservation.

There is a story that the emperor Shah Jahan, who visited Kashmir in 1633, " decided that the garden was altogether too splendid for a subject, even though that subject might happen to be his own prime minister and father-in-law. He told Asaf Khan on three occasions how much he admired his pleasure-ground, expecting that it would be immediately offered for the royal acceptance. But if Shah Jahan coveted his neighbour's vine-yard, the Wazir was a no less stiff-necked Naboth; he could not bring himself to surrender his cherished pleasaunce to be ' a garden of herbs ' for his royal master, and he remained silent. Then as now, the same stream supplied both the Royal Garden (Shahlimar) and Nishat Bagh, which lies on the mountain-side between Shalimar and the city of Srinagar. So Shah Jahan in his anger ordered the water-supply to be cut off from Nishat Bagh, and was avenged, for the garden he envied was shorn of all its beauty.

" Nothing is more desolate than one of these great enclosures when their stone-lined tanks and water channels are dry and empty. Asaf Khan, who was staying in his summer palace at the time, could do nothing, and all his household knew of his grief and bitter disappointment. One day, lost in a melancholy reverie, he at last fell fast asleep in the shade by the empty water-course. At length a noise aroused him; rubbing his eyes, he could hardly believe what he saw, for the fountains were all playing merrily once more and the long carved water-chutes were white with foam. A faithful servant, risking his life, had defied the Emperor's orders, and removed the obstruction from the stream. Asaf Khan rebuked him for his zeal and hastily had the stream closed again. But the news reached the Emperor in his gardens at Shalimar; whereupon he sent for the terri-fied servant and, much to the surprise of the Court, instead of punishing him, bestowed a robe of honour upon him to mark his admiration for this act of devoted service; at the same time granting a sanad which gave the right to his master to draw water from the garden from the Shalimar stream."[1]

SHALIMAR

Shalimar is, of all the Mughal gardens in Kashmir, the one which has received the greatest attention from the later rulers of the country. The Pathan and the Sikh Governors occasionally used it as their pleasure resort, and when, from the reign of Ranjit Singh, Europeans began to visit the valley with comparative freedom, its marble pavilion was often assigned to them as a residence. But in spite of this inter-mittent care, the destroying hand of time and the wanton vandalism of some of the rulers themselves have robbed the summer residence of Nur Jahan and Jahangir of a great part of its ancient charm. An idea of what it was in the time of the Mughals may be gathered from the tantalisingly short description of François Bernier, who visited Kashmir in the suite of Aurangzeb in A.D. 1664:—

" The most beautiful of all these gardens is one belonging to the king, called Chah-limar. The entrance from the lake is through a spacious canal bordered with green turf and running between two rows of poplars. The length is about five hundred paces, and it leads

---

[1] Mrs. Villiers-Stuart, *Gardens of the Great Mughals*, pp. 168-170.

to a large summer-house placed in the middle of the garden. A second canal, still finer than the first, then conducts to another summer-house at the end of the garden. This canal is paved with large blocks of freestone and its sloping sides are covered with the same. In the middle is a long row of fountains, fifteen paces apart; besides which there are here and there large circular basins or reservoirs, out of which arise other fountains, formed into a variety of shapes and figures.

" The summer-houses are placed in the midst of the canal, consequently surrounded by water and between the two rows of large poplars planted on either side. They are built in the form of a dome, and encircled by a gallery, into which four doors open; two looking up or down the canal and two leading to bridges that connect the buildings with both banks. The houses consist of a large room in the centre with four smaller apartments, one at each corner. The whole of the interior is painted and gilt, and on the walls of all the chambers are inscribed certain sentences written in large and beautiful Persian characters.[1]

" The four doors are extremely valuable; being composed of large stones and supported by two beautiful pillars. The doors and pillars were found in some of the idol temples demolished by Shah Jahan and it is impossible to estimate their value. I cannot describe the nature of the stone, but it is far superior to porphyry or any species of marble."[2]

The large stone doors now no longer exist; the domes have given place to a common shingle roof; the gilding and paint and the inscription on the walls are now covered or replaced by a coat of whitewash; the view of the lake is cut off by an ugly stone wall; but in spite of these disastrous changes, the garden still preserves its singular charm. In strong contrast with the buoyant atmosphere of Nishat Bagh, with its sunlit terraces, its dashing cascades, playing

---

[1] Among other inscriptions, the celebrated legend: *agar firdaus bar ru-e zamin ast, hamin ast o hamin ast o hamin ast.* (If there be a paradise on earth, it is this, it is this, it is this).

[2] Bernier, pp. 399-400.

fountains and sparkling streams, is the soft gloom and the gliding motion of the water-courses of the Shalimar, which is built on a comparatively flat piece of ground. The garden was a royal residence, and the court seems to have indelibly imprinted its spirit of decorum upon it. As the garden was probably designed by the Empress Nur Jahan, who in point of beauty and wit was the most pre-eminent lady in Muslim India, it would, perhaps, be more appropriate to say that the garden reflects the image of that queen of the harem, whom her fond lover designated the Light of the World.

The garden originally consisted, as now, of three enclosures, the lower one of which, however, has been considerably curtailed by the intrusion of the cart-road. The outermost enclosure was used as the public garden, and its *barahdari* was the Diwan-i-Am (the Hall of Public Audience). The small black marble throne still stands over the water-fall in the centre of the canal which flows through the building into the tank below.

" The second garden is slightly broader, consisting of two shallow terraces with the Diwan-i-Khas (the Hall of Private Audience) in the centre. The buildings have been destroyed, but their carved stone bases are left, as well as a fine platform surrounded by fountains. On the north-west boundary of this enclosure are the royal bath-rooms.

" At the next wall, the little guard-rooms that flank the entrance to the ladies' garden have been rebuilt in Kashmir style on older stone bases. Here the whole effect culminates with the beautiful black marble pavilion built by Shah Jahan, which still stands in the midst of its fountain spray; the green glitter of the water shining in the smooth, polished marble, the deep rich tone of which is repeated in the old cypress trees. Round this baradari the whole colour and perfume of the garden is concentrated, with the snows of Mahadev for a background. How well the Mughals understood the principle that the garden, like every other work of art, should have a climax (Plate XIV).

" This unique pavilion is surrounded on every side by a series of cascades, and at night when the lamps are lighted in the little arched recesses behind the shining waterfalls it is even more fairy-like than by day."[1]

HARWAN EXCAVATIONS

(For Site Plan see Plate LXXVII)

Harwan is the name of a small village situated about 2 miles beyond the Shalimar garden. The only distinction it at present enjoys is derived from its being the site of the head-works of the magnificent water-supply system of Srinagar. Though the name Harwan had been identified by Sir Aurel Stein with Shadar-hadvana (grove of six saints), a locality mentioned in the *Raja-tarangini*, there were no indications above ground pointing to the existence of important monuments buried under the earth. It is true that over thirty years ago a few moulded brick tiles had been exhumed in the course of construction of the conduit which carries drinking-water to Srinagar; but as these were merely stray fragments no efforts were made to trace their origin. It is only recently that this much-delayed task has been undertaken.

Fortunately, at the very outset, the enquiry was facilitated by a lucky chance. It was on a brilliant afternoon that the site was first surveyed. The hill-side along which the water conduit runs was waving with long-stalked Indian corn. But amid all those fields of luxuriant corn there existed a square flat patch which was covered only with thin turf, and in which there grew a solitary stunted plane tree. This plot of land, by reason of its apparent unproductiveness, immediately attracted attention. On enquiry from the neat-herd who was watering his cattle in the brook near by, it was ascertained that this barren field owned the significant name of Kitur-i-Daj (field of potsherds), because the entire field consisted of thickly packed sherds—whence its barrenness. The question that naturally arose was how such an abundance of potsherds could occur so high

[1] Mrs. Villiers-Stuart, *Gardens of the Great Mughals*, p. 163 *et seq.*

up the hill-side and so far from the present inhabited areas.   The only explanation (which eventually turned out to be correct) was that in ancient times there had been dwellings here—dwellings the nature of which could be ascertained only by excavation.

Within a few days of the commencement of the excavation a number of walls came to light (Plate XV).   They were ordinary rubble stone structures, at first sight scarcely distinguishable from the modern mud-and-stone walls of peasants' dwellings in Kashmir.   When the operations had advanced, it was discovered that there was a method in the arrangement of the stones—*e.g.*, a number of large boulders was placed in one row with intervening spaces between each pair of them.   These spaces were filled with smaller stones, so that the entire façade presented a diaper effect.   None of these stones was dressed.   This style of construction was given the name " diaper rubble " style (Plate XVI).   Among the buildings constructed in this style are (1) the triple base of a medium-sized stupa, and (2) a set of rooms which might have served as chapels, or for residential purposes. The stupa is built in the middle of a rectangular courtyard facing north.   While digging under its foundations a copper coin of Toramana, the White Hun ruler, who flourished in about the fifth century A.D., was discovered.   From this piece of evidence it was inferred that the " diaper rubble " stupa could not possibly be earlier than the fifth century A.D., though it might be considerably later in date.

Immediately around the stupa there was a narrow fringe of figured-tile pavement.   A close examination of it showed that (1) nearly all the pieces were fragmentary; (2) though nearly all of them bore figures, no group of adjacent pieces completed a motif; and (3) though some were flat and might have formed part of a pavement, there were a few which bore mouldings in relief and could only have belonged to walls.   The obvious inference was that these tiles were transplanted from a different structure, probably earlier, when that structure had fallen into desuetude.   The question now was to find the structure to which they originally belonged.

In this area, however, the rubble stone structures—*e.g.*, the stupa and the chapels—were not the only buildings that were exhumed. Side by side with them were other buildings in quite different styles— for example, two adjacent walls of what might have been the court- yard of some edifice of which no trace came to light.   These walls had a core of rubble stones, but their facing consisted of closely packed small pebbles, transported from the bed of the neighbouring torrent.   The walls are built entirely in mud, but the pebbles are so carefully packed that after the lapse of nearly two thousand years the portion of the wall that remains standing presents a very neat appearance.   But the labour involved in collecting and fixing such small pebbles in an extensive building must have been enormous. This style of construction has, for want of a better name, been termed the " pebble " style (Plate XVII).   Again, another enclosure wall in a far better state of preservation was found.   This is built in a peculiar style, which is evidently a cross between the older pebble style and the later rubble style, and provides a strikingly effective façade (Plate XIX).   It consists of a series of large, smooth-faced, irregularly shaped boulders placed at intervals of 6″ to 18″ apart, the interspaces being filled with small round or oval pebbles of 1″ to 2″ in diameter.   It appears that the builders' solicitude for the durability of their buildings in time overcame their desire to acquire religious merit by devoting extra, though unnecessary, labour in the construc- tion of religious buildings.

Among the antiquities that this area yielded, were a large number of broken fingers and toes of terra-cotta figures, terra-cotta curls belonging to images of the Buddha, of which no other remnant was found, and a few clay votive tablets bearing in relief miniature stupas. These last are extremely interesting, inasmuch as they give an idea of the kind of stupas that were built in Kashmir in the early centuries of the Christian era.   The stupa depicted on the tablets had a triple base, all the three flights of steps leading up being in line with one another, as is the case with the existing stupa at Harwan.   From the uppermost basement sprang a cylindrical dome with a bulging hemispherical top, which was surmounted by a number of umbrellas, standing one over the other, and diminishing in size until they end in a pointed finial.   They are supported by what appears to be a forest of poles radiating outwards.   To the finial were attached several long waving streamers.   On one side of the stupa, standing in the courtyard, or it may be on the first terrace of the plinth, was a "lion" column.   Below the representation of the stupa on the plaque, the Buddhist creed, *Ye dharma*, etc., in Brahmi characters of about the fourth century A.D., is stamped in relief (Plate XVIII).

A closer scrutiny of the hill-side brought to light the fact that in the period to which the ruins belong it was arranged in level terraces, on each of which stood several buildings.   There was a central flight of steps which connected them, and gave access from one to the other. It is likely that it was continued to the foot of the hill, along which runs a beautiful stream of clear water, although the shrines were not wholly dependent for their drinking water upon the stream.   There exist to this day two springs, one above and the other near the ruins, and probably in the old days there was a larger number.

On the highest of these terraces, which, by the way, grew excellent corn at the time of excavation, there was a little mound whose general appearance seemed promising.   Nor did the operations, carried out later, belie that promise, for they brought to light the most important of the buildings so far exhumed at this site.   It is a large apsidal temple, square in front and circular at the back, built in the very picturesque diaper pebble style of masonry.   The temple accommodation consisted of a spacious rectangular antechamber with a circular sanctum behind.   No relic of any kind nor any trace of an image was found, but this deficiency was made up by the wonderful pavement of the courtyard round the temple, consisting of large moulded brick tiles having various shapes and forming different patterns (Plate XIX).   The favourite pattern seems to have been a large disc consisting of several concentric circles with a single central piece.

Each circle is composed of a series of arc-shaped tiles, each stamped with a special motif. The principal motifs on the tiles so far discovered are (1) designs consisting of frets, wavy lines, fish-bone patterns, conventional flowers, and flower-designs consisting of different combinations of leaves; (2) leaves of an aquatic plant common in the neighbouring Dal lake; leaves of the lotus plant, some indigenous flowers in full bloom grouped in various ways; (3) geese running or flying in rows with flower petals or leaves in their bills; ducks; cocks or pheasants often placed in the centre of a floral pattern; cocks fighting; (4) rams fighting; cows suckling their young; elephants; deer looking with head turned backwards at the moon; archers on horseback chasing deer and shooting arrows at them; (5) a lady carrying a flower vase; a dancing girl; a female musician beating a drum; a soldier in armour hunting deer with bow and arrow; men and women conversing, seated in a balcony; boys carrying a floral festoon on their shoulders. That these tiles occupied exactly the position they were laid in by ancient workmen is borne out by the fact that each one of them bears a number in Kharoshthi script, the order of the tiles in a series being in strict accordance with their consecutive numeral order. The obvious inference is that the tile-pavement was not laid in a haphazard manner, but followed a set design, probably drawn first by the architect on paper or parchment. The potter who made the tiles and stamped them with decorative figures numbered them before baking, to prevent the comparatively unskilled layer from making mistakes and thereby spoiling the design. Incidentally it shows that in ancient India, over fifteen centuries ago, labourers were expected to know at least the rudiments of writing and reading. The existence of Kharoshthi numerals also affords a reliable clue to the date of the tiles, and consequently to that of the monuments. Kharoshthi script ceased to be in vogue in north-western India, where it had principally flourished, about the fifth century A.D. It follows therefore that the tiles belong to a period anterior to that century, possibly a con-

siderable period. The fact that the Kharoshthi numerals at Harwan
were intended for the guidance of common labourers indicates that
the script must have been at the highest pitch of popularity at the
time the tiles were made. I should accordingly place the date of
the tiles, and consequently that of the diaper pebble masonry
with which they are associated, at about A.D. 300. This conclusion
receives further support from the style of the human figures and other
designs stamped on the tiles. For example, the physiognomy and,
to some extent, the dress of the men and women are wholly unlike
that of any of the races at present residing in Kashmir, or for the
matter of that in India. Their facial characteristics bear close
resemblance to those of inhabitants of the regions round about
Yarkand and Kashgar, whose heavy features prominent cheek-
bones, narrow, sunk, and slanting eyes, and receding foreheads, are
faithfully represented on the tiles. Some of the figures are dressed
in trousers and Turkoman caps. The only period when Kashmir
had any intimate connection with Central Asia was during the
supremacy of the Kushans in the early centuries of the Christian era,
when Kashmir formed part of the Kushan empire, which extended
from Mathura in India to Yarkand in Central Asia. Indeed, then
as now it appears to have occupied a pre-eminent position; inasmuch
as Kanishka (circa A.D. 125), the greatest of Kushan emperors, is
said to have convened here his great council of Buddhist divines.
It may be that some pious and prosperous Kushan built this shrine
at Harwan, where, according to the ancient history of Kashmir,
resided the great Buddhist patriarch, Nagarjuna. Further perhaps
to increase his religious merit, and to show his humility, the builder
had the image of his own face and that of his wife's stamped on the
tiles so that the commonest people might tread on them. Among
the other decorative motifs which reveal foreign influence are the
figures of mailed horsemen with flying scarves tied to their heads,
which are strongly reminiscent of the contemporary Sassanian art of
Persia.

The tile decoration was not confined to the pavement only. Though very few moulded tiles belonging to the façade have been found, their fragments prove that, up to a certain height at least, the façade also was decorated with tile-work. This is further borne out by the discovery of a long platform at the back of the courtyard, which almost throughout its length bears such decoration (Plate XXI).

The peculiar interest of the Harwan monuments lies in the fact that they are the only remains of their kind in India (possibly in the world), and that they supply a life-like representation of the features of those mysterious people, the Kushans.

From the above it is clear that the pebble style of buildings was the earliest in date. It was followed by the diaper pebble style, which dates about A.D. 300. This style was followed by the diaper rubble style, whose date is about A.D. 500 and later.

The dimensions of the tile pavement round the apsidal temple are 160′ by 124′ 6″. The tiles, as stated above, are decorated with a variety of motifs, the most prominent of which are reproduced in the accompanying illustrations. It will be noticed that a striking feature of the human figures on the tiles is that the head is invariably shown in profile and the body facing front (Plates XX-XLII).

YANDRAHOM MEGALITHS

From the Harwan ruins, looking north-west, may be seen, situated on the plateau of Burzahom, 2 miles away, the only pre-historic remains, save stone implements, which have so far been discovered in Kashmir. They consist of a group of eleven megaliths, five of which are more or less erect: the rest have fallen. As no excavations have yet been carried out at this site, it is impossible to state precisely what they are and to what period they belong (Plate XLIII).

V

MONUMENTS ABOVE SRINAGAR

Srinagar to Pandrethan	3½ miles	Motor road	
Srinagar to Avantipur	18 miles	Motor road	
Srinagar to Loduv	16 miles	Road partly unmetalled	
Avantipur to Payar and back	12 miles	Bridle-path	
Avantipur to Narastan	20 miles	Bridle-path	Tents and necessaries must be taken
Srinagar to Martand	39 miles	Motor road	Rest House at Matan
Srinagar to Achhabal	39 miles	Motor road	Dak Bungalow at Achhabal
Achhabal to Kother and back	6 miles	Motor road and bridle-path	
Martand to Mamal, two stages	30 miles	Motor road to Pahalgam, opposite to which, across the stream, is Mamal	
Martand and Bumzu and back	2 miles	Motor road	
Srinagar to Verinag	50 miles	Motor road	Dak Bungalow at Munda within 5 miles

PANDRETHAN

The small village of Pandrethan[1] is situated 3 miles above Srinagar on the Anantnag cart-road. At present its only attraction, excepting the newly built military barracks, is the well-preserved mediæval temple behind the willow grove on the left-hand side of the cart-road (Plates XLIV, LXIII, LXIV, LXV and LXVI). The temple measures 17′ 6″ square externally, and belongs to the *maṇḍapa* type—*i.e.*, it is open on all the four sides. The unusually bold projection of the pilasters which support the pediments of the porches is "a great improvement upon the earlier stage, as the boldness of the projection and the retirement of the connecting

[1] Since the above was written, the village has been removed.

112

walls afford a great and pleasing variety of light and shade which is altogether wanting in some parts of the more ancient buildings."[1] The roof is of the usual pyramidal type, but its monotony is relieved by an ornamental band of dentils which divides it horizontally into two storeys.   In the upper section of the pyramid are four trefoiled ventilation apertures which remind one forcibly of similar niches in the architecture of Gandhara.   The interior of the cella is plain, except for the ceiling (Plate LXVI), which is one of the best examples of carving on stone extant in Kashmir.   It consists of nine stones arranged in three overlapping squares, each of which cuts off the angles of the square below it, and thus reduces the extent of the space to be covered.   The twelve triangles so formed have been utilised for figure decoration.   Each triangle in the lowest square contains a pair of flying Yakshas, facing each other and holding a garland in their hands, which falls in swags about their bodies and between their knees.   The second group of triangles contains only four figures, each holding a disc in his right hand and a lotus stalk in his left.   Underneath his right arm is seen the outstretched end of flying drapery.   The uppermost set of triangles contains a similar group of flying figures.   The whole is crowned by a square slab decorated with an exquisitely carved full-blown lotus within a beaded circle.   The convention by which the peculiarly graceful floating motion of the body, somewhat similar to that of a swimmer, is made to represent the flight of human figures without the appendage of wings, is noteworthy.   The floor of the cella is paved with stone flags.   In the centre is the depression about 7′ square which must have held the pedestal of the image worshipped in the temple.

The plinth of the temple remains submerged for the greater part of the year, but it is certain that it is well preserved.   A remarkable feature of it is the string-course of elephants which runs round the temple and upon which the walls of the sanctum rest.   The springs which have arisen round the structure do not seem to have

[1] Cunningham, *J.A.S.B.*, 1848, part ii, p. 286.

8

been there when the temple was originally built, for it is impossible to believe, now that Cunningham's theory of " the Kashmirian temple being placed in the centre of a tank " no longer holds good, that the temple was built in the midst of an extensive marsh, which has only lately been drained.

Cunningham, and after him Cowie, Cole, etc., believed that the temple was " Vishnu-meruvardhanasvami," built by Meruvardhana, the minister of Partha who flourished in the beginning of the tenth century A.D. He bases his identification on the statement of the *Rajatarangini* coupled with absence of other temples in Pandrethan. But this theory is considerably weakened by the presence, in the trefoiled niche above the northern entrance, of a seated figure which is believed to be the Lakuliśa form of Śiva, and by the internal arrangement of the floor of the cella which " can only admit of a Śiva image." The *Rajatarangini* mentions in another passage[1] the erection of the temple of Śiva-Rilhaneśvara by Rilhana, the minister of Jayasimha, about the year A.D. 1135. There is nothing in the architectural style against the identification of our temple with Rilhana's foundation.

Around this site a number of late Brahmanical images have been found.

Buddhist Remains at Pandrethan

But the history of Pandrethan goes much farther back than the twelfth century A.D. The name is a corruption of Puranadhisthana, which means " Old Capital." It was founded under the name of Śrinagari by the emperor Aśoka in the third century B.C. But eight hundred years after, Pravarasena II removed the site of his capital farther down the river. Gradually the younger city not only deprived its older rival of all its importance, but usurped its name also, and Aśoka's city came to be known simply by the appellation of

---

[1] *Rajat.*, vol. ii, verses 2408-9. The greater part of the temple has now been cleared by the excavation of a drain all round it.

Puranadhishthana (old city). This name was in use as early as the time of Hsüan-tsang (seventh century A.D.). The only remains that now exist of the ancient Pandrethan are the ruins of level terraces, long lines of loose rubble walls, and innumerable mounds of stone debris, which thickly dot the mountain slopes from Pantchhok to the Śankaracharya hill—an extent of about 2 miles. Not all these heaps of debris, however, are expected to conceal ancient remains. In fact, a considerable number of them appear to have been collected together for the purpose of bringing all available land under cultivation in olden times, when the population of the country seems to have been larger than it is now. But there are a good many the excavation of which will undoubtedly yield interesting results. Three such mounds have been tapped and have revealed two Buddhist stupas and the courtyard of a monastery. They are situated on the mountain slope about half a mile to the east of the temple.

The stupa known in the records of the Archæological Department of the State as " Stupa A " is the larger of the two. It was surrounded by a dressed stone wall, only the lowest course of which exists in places. The entrance to the compound seems to have been in the middle of the south wall. The stupa has lost its outer dressed stone casing, except in one or two places. These, however, are sufficient to show that it was in plan a square of 72′ with offsets on each side, the re-entering angles of which must have afforded a pleasing contrast of light and shade. Almost all that exists at present is the circular rubble stone core of the structure.

To the west of it is another stupa, but it has been so carefully demolished that nothing remains of it except a few stones, and a rail of its western stair.

With the exception of a few fragmentary sculptures which may be assigned to about the seventh century A.D. or perhaps a little earlier, nothing of importance was found at these sites. The sculptures are, however, very interesting inasmuch as they show that the influence of the art of the Imperial Guptas had penetrated into Kashmir and left a permanent mark upon the local craftsmanship. These sculptures are now in the Srinagar Museum. Plate XLV illustrates a life-size image of a Bodhisattva excavated at Pandrethan. While digging for the foundations of the military buildings in the new cantonment near by, nearly a dozen beautiful sculptures, more than life-size, representing Indrani, Chamunda, Varahi, and other goddesses, known as the Ashta-matrika (eight mothers) were discovered. These too are now preserved in the Srinagar Museum.

The ruins mentioned above and the Śiva temple show that the old capital, though eclipsed by its younger rival, was not entirely deserted even in the later centuries of the mediæval epoch. Another ancient relic is the beautifully carved stone capital (Plate LXVII) built into a late Muslim platform, situated on the hill slope towards the east of the temple. The carving consists of a pair of geese with highly ornamental foliated tails and crests, facing each other and pecking at what looks like a bunch of grapes placed upon a decorative stand.

PAMPUR

The flourishing town of Pampur was founded in the beginning of the ninth century A.D. by Padma, who, though the son of a spirit distiller, had through the influence of his sister, a concubine of King Lalitaditya and mother of the minor Chippata-Jayapida, risen to the position of an all-powerful minister. He consecrated the temple of Padmasvami-Vishnu at Pampur, ancient Padmapura. Remains of the cella of a temple are still in existence near the shrine of Shah Hamadan, which has appropriated two of its fluted columns and other carved stones. Probably these fragments are all that remain of Padma's temple.

The mosque of Pampur is an inferior imitation of the ziarat (shrine) of Shah Hamadan in Srinagar (Plate XLVI).

LODUV

Three miles and a half above Pandrethan, the road branches off to the sulphur springs at Wuyan and the Khruv game preserves.

The branch road skirts the foot of the hills, and after describing a wide sweep of nearly 10 miles, joins the main road at Barus. The village of Loduv is situated on this road at a distance of 3 miles from the last-mentioned place. It contains two temples, the larger one (Plate XLVII) of which stands in the middle of a shallow tank of water which is fed by a spring in its north-east corner. The temple is a very simple structure 24′ square externally. It differs from every other temple of Kashmir both in plan and in appearance. Externally the walls are without decoration, their bareness being only partially relieved by a cornice which consists of three courses of stone adorned with projecting fillets. There is a torus course at the base. The corner pilasters are quite plain, and project only very slightly from the walls. The entrance, which is on the south-west side, is headed by a semicircular, almost horseshoe-shaped, arch surmounted by a single-storied pediment of very slight projection. Internally the temple is circular with a diameter of 17′ 6″. In this respect it resembles the Sankaracharya temple on the Takht-i Sulaiman hill. The wall surfaces are quite plain. At a height of nearly 10′ from the ground level is a plain projecting string-course over which springs the domical ceiling. The dome was built of projecting courses of *kanjur* in lime, and must have been similar to the ceiling of the larger temples at Wangath. The holes and mortices in the walls seem to have been intended for scaffolding while the temple was under construction.

The simplicity of its plan and decoration seems to point to its being, perhaps, the oldest example[1] of Kashmiri mediæval architecture and the prototype of the elaborate style which culminated at Martand and Avantipur.

The water of the tank is nowhere more than a few inches deep, and a number of green fish of a remarkably light and transparent tinge may always be seen swimming gracefully in it.

[1] For a discussion of its place in Kashmiri architecture, see the chapter on Architectural Styles.

A few yards behind this temple, higher up the hill and immediately at the back of the mosque, is a smaller temple which externally presents nearly the same appearance as the larger temple, the only difference being that the projecting pediment which enclosed the round-headed doorway has here developed into a well-defined portico with a trefoil niche. From this arrangement there is but a single easy step to the full trefoil-headed recess or entrance enclosed in a steep pediment which is so universal a feature of the mediæval religious edifices of Kashmir. As a matter of fact the portico of this same temple had a true trefoiled arch, of which the lower courses are still extant. Internally the temple is only 6′ square. The ceiling consists of three courses of overlapping stones. There is a base for the image in the centre. The corner pilasters project not more than 2″. They are surmounted by rectangular capitals, which seem to have originally borne in relief the figures of some animals, probably lions, standing back to back. The capitals of the pilasters of the portico are carved with floral scrolls.

AVANTIPUR

Avantiśvara Temple

The village of Avantipur, situated at a distance of 18 miles from Srinagar on the Anantnag cart-road, represents the town of Avantipura, founded by Avantivarman, who reigned from A.D. 855 to 883. Its chief interest centres in two magnificent temples with which its founder embellished it. The first and larger is the temple of Śiva-Avantiśvara, whose massive walls rise in forlorn grandeur outside the village of Jaubror, half a mile below Avantipur. The temple, which has been sadly mutilated, is situated in a courtyard enclosed by a massive stone wall, the western face of which is adorned externally with a row of fluted columns, but without any recesses behind. The gateway is in the middle of this wall, and is divided into two chambers by a cross wall. Its walls are not decorated with figure sculpture. The niches and the panels are quite plain.

The base on which the shrine in the centre of the courtyard stands is 57′ 4″ square and 10′ high. To each of its corners was attached a platform about 16′ square, which must originally have supported a small subsidiary shrine. It has a stair on each of its four sides like the temple of Pandrethan. The stairs have a width of 28½′, and are supported on either side by flank walls 17½′ in length. The sanctum has been reduced to a "confused mass of ruins."

The platforms seem to have originally been attached to the plinth of the temple at one point only, but afterwards they were completely joined with it by means of a connecting wall built of architectural fragments which had fallen from the temple. This arrangement can best be seen at the south-eastern corner of the base.

The sole exterior decoration of the temple base, the only part of the building that exists, is a series of projecting facets, the larger of which were originally surmounted by plain rectangular capitals.

In the two rear corners of the courtyard are two subsidiary shrines.

There is a large assortment of architectural fragments strewn about in the courtyard, the most interesting of which are (1) the spandrel of an arch in front of the southern stair, (2) the flower-and-vase capital of a dodecagonal pilaster, (3) the spandrel of another arch by its side, and (4) the base of a pilaster decorated with two seated rams and a dancing girl who plays upon a *ḍamaru* (small hand-drum) standing on a throne ornamented with two lions at the sides and an elephant, facing, in the middle.

Avantisvami Temple

Half a mile farther up is the small but much more ornate and better preserved temple of Avantisvami-Vishnu. It is the work of

Avantivarman's youth, before he came to the throne. It has been reclaimed by the removal of an enormous mass of silt and débris which during a thousand years of neglect (for the temple had already silted up when it suffered from the iconoclasts) had accumulated to a height of about 15′ and buried the whole structure except the upper part of the walls of the gateway and a shapeless heap of stones in the centre.

The edifice comprises a colonnaded peristyle (Plates XLVIII and XLIX) enclosing a paved courtyard 174′ by 148′ 8″, in the centre of which is the main shrine, built on a double base with four smaller shrines at the four corners. The peristyle is comparatively plain externally except on the west side, which has a row of fluted columns. The only decoration on the other three sides is a rectangular string-course and pilasters enclosing rectangular spaces, corresponding respectively with the cyma recta cornice of the plinth and the cells inside. The entrance, which is in the middle of the west wall, is divided by a cross-wall into two chambers, and is approached by a flight of steps bounded on either side by a plain rail and a side-wall. The front pilasters of the side-walls bear figures of Vishnu and of his consorts carved in relief. On either side of it was a portico supported on tall massive advanced columns, one of which exists to this day, though in a precarious condition.

The wall surface of the entrance is both externally and internally ornamented profusely with sculptured reliefs (Plate L). The larger female figures on the right and left hand walls of the outer chamber represent the goddesses Ganga and Yamuna, easily recognised by their respective vehicles, the crocodile (*makara*) and the tortoise. The scenes in the rectangular panel on the right-hand pilaster of the wall represent probably a king and his two queens seated in "sportive fashion" on a *simhāsana* (lion throne), here symbolised by two lions facing, one on each side of the panel. On the two external sides of this pilaster the scenes are the same with slight variations. In the scene in front the lions have been replaced by two standing females. In the southern panel the king has his right hand in the *abhayamudrā* (attitude of granting immunity from fear), and the lady on his right is admiring her own charms, reflected in a round pocket-mirror which she holds in her right hand. In the other two panels the figures are seated on separate cushions; here all three occupy a single long cushion.

Three rectangular panels are carved on the huge block which forms the lowest course of the left wall of the gateway. The largest panel is in the middle and contains a bas-relief. In the centre are three figures, a male and two female *chauri* [1]-bearers; but much more interesting are the highly caparisoned elephants who are fighting with horned birds of monstrous size. It is evident that the elephant is fighting at a disadvantage. (Perhaps the scene symbolises the fight of Garuda with the Nagas, the latter here being represented by the elephants and not the usual snake gods. Naga means both snake and elephant.) The other two scenes contain each a male figure standing with folded hands between two human-headed birds. Above this is a row of *kīrtimukhas*, or lions' heads, surmounted by a line of rosettes. Higher still is another row of circular panels, each containing a Garuda. The rectangular panel in the left cross-wall contains a male and two female figures seated on a cushioned sofa in a grove of trees. They seem to be in a joyous mood. The man is offering the lady at his left hand what seems to be a cup of wine, while the doves at their feet are billing and cooing in sympathy. Above the group is a pedimental niche which contains a smaller representation of the goddess Ganga. On the narrow facets on either side of this niche is a vertical row of standing pairs of male and female figures. This row starts from a rectangular panel which contains the figure of a four-armed Atlas wearing a cushion-like head-dress. The walls were decorated with numerous groups of figures, but unfortunately most of them are now too defaced to be distinguished, much less identified.

[1] *Chauri* is a flywhisk made of the tail of a *yak*.

The view of the courtyard from the inner chamber of the gateway is charming.   In place of the bald monotony of the external surface of the peristyle, the eye feasts on all sides on the picturesque ruins of a beautiful range of cells, preceded by a noble row of fluted columns. Another flight of steps similar to that on the outside leads down to the stone-paved courtyard.   The side-walls of this stair are plain, but the pilasters are covered with sculptured reliefs.   Each of the smaller panels facing the courtyard depicts an erotic scene.

In the middle of the space between the gateway and the main shrine is a stepped stone which appears to be the base of a Garuda-dhvaja.   It will be remembered that Garuda, the divine eagle, is the vehicle of Vishnu, and also forms the emblem on the banner of his Master.   Thus the Garuda-dhvaja column is always an indispensable adjunct of Vaishnava temples.

The central shrine is built on a double base, the only decoration of which is a torus moulding and a cyma recta cornice (Plate LXXIV). The base is intact, but the sanctum, which measured 33′ square externally, has almost disappeared.   In fact the only fragments remaining are some parts of the lowest courses and a few stones of the north wall.

Unlike its sister temple lower down the road, this edifice has only one stair.   But that apparent deficiency is more than rectified by the sculptured reliefs on its pilasters.   The two scenes facing the gateway represent Vishnu, the deity worshipped in the temple, seated in an easy attitude between his two consorts, Lakshmi and Bhumi (?).   Lakshmi in the northern group (Plate L) is distinguished by the cornucopia which, even in the late ninth century, to which this temple belongs, was retained as the special emblem of the goddess, who traces her descent, through Gandhara, from the Greek Athene. Vishnu in the northern relief possesses six arms, two of which, in impartial affection, encircle the bodies of his two consorts, while the remaining four hold his distinctive emblems, the bow, the mace, and the lotus, etc.   Below the throne are two pairs of parrots, and the same bird crowns the capitals of the square pilasters from which springs the cusped arch which canopies the divine group. The panel is surmounted by a dentil course consisting of conventional lions' heads (*kīrtimukhas*) alternating with geese and flowers. This again is surmounted by a border of square rosettes (Plates L and LXX, A).

The group on the opposite pilaster is similar to that described above, the main difference being that the god, instead of having six has only four arms. The goddesses in every case have only two arms. Both the god and the goddesses are elaborately ornamented. The former has his hair brushed neatly back and arranged in braids which are tied in knots on the top. Two roses are inserted in the braids just above the ears. Besides the necklace and armlets he wears the *mandaramala* (garland of celestial flowers). An enormous circular ornamental disc adorns his right ear, while a smaller jewelled pendant is suspended from his left ear. The goddesses, whose exaggerated breasts and attenuated waists are even more profusely ornamented, are crowned with three-peaked tiaras. Their ear-lobes are unusually elongated by the weight of their heavy circular ear ornaments.

The relief on the inner surface of the southern pilaster represents a group of ten figures, the central and the largest pair consisting of a male and a female wearing *dhotis*. The male wears an ornamental band across his breast (over his right shoulder and under his left arm). The whole group seems to breathe a spirit of profound devotion to some undefined object. It probably represents the major and minor gods coming to worship the image of Vishnu in the temple.

The group opposite also comprises ten persons. The principal figures are those of a bearded and crowned male, probably representing the donor, and a lady, perhaps the princess, who wears a scarf over her head which hangs low down her shoulders, a fashion which the women of Kashmir have preserved to this day. The lady is followed by a female attendant. Above her is a male, who wears a curiously knotted and twisted head-dress.

The courtyard is paved with stone flags, and measures 174′ east to west by 148′ 8″ north to south. The five shrines in the courtyard, arranged in a quincunx, show that the group was intended to belong to the *pañcharatna* (five jewels) class. The shrine in the north-east corner seems to have been dedicated to the river goddess Ganga, as the spout of the pedestal of the image which it contained has been carved in the shape of a *makara*, or crocodile, which is the vehicle of that goddess. The water trough in the courtyard on the north side of the main shrine was intended to hold the sacred washings of the deity inside the sanctum.

But the chief beauty of the temple lies in its cellular colonnade (Plates XLVIII, LXVIII, and LXIX). It comprises sixty-nine cells, each of which measures on the average 3′ 8″ by 4′ 10″, the cell in the centre on each side being larger than the rest and advanced slightly forwards. All of them are preceded by twenty-four-sided columns on plain square bases which have for the most part suffered severely at the hands of the destroyer. The only wall decoration of the peristyle is the range of 138 half-engaged columns (Plates LXXI and LXXII) on the pilasters on both sides of the trefoiled entrance of the cells. The latter were intended to contain replicas of the main image which the temple enshrined. In one or two of them in the eastern wall of the peristyle the pedestals of these images are still found *in situ*.

A large assortment of antiquities has been unearthed during the excavation of this temple. The most valuable are a series of sculptures which have been placed in the Srinagar Museum.[1] The large jars arranged in a row on the lawn above the excavations were, doubtless, used for the storage of grain and foodstuffs. Among those that have been brought to the Museum is one which bears an inscription mentioning the name of Avantivarman. This record is of interest as being the only independent evidence of the correct identification of the site.

Kalhana states that the Avantisvami temple was occasionally

---

[1] See handbook of the Archæological and Numismatic Sections of the Sri Pratap Singh Museum, Srinagar.

subjected to sacrilegious treatment even in Hindu times. The tyrannical Kalaśa[1] (A.D. 1081-1089) confiscated the villages which formed its endowments. Its military possibilities do not seem to have escaped the notice of the ancients, for " its courtyard served as a fortification when, shortly after the accession of King Jayasimha (A.D. 1128), Bhasa, a commander of the royal troops, was besieged at Avantipur by the rebel Damaras of the Holada (Vular) district."[2] In the fourteenth century Sikandar But-shikan completed the destruction which had already begun in the troublous times which followed the reign of Avantivarman.

MALANGPURA

Halfway between Avantipur and Payar, about 3 miles from each, is the village of Malangpura, partly hidden from the highroad by the projecting spur of the *karewa*. On the top of this spur are the ruins of a mediæval stupa, the only part of which that is in position being the base. The stupa follows the usual plan of other similar structures of its age in Kashmir in that it is square, with two projections on either side and large staircases each of which faces a cardinal point. The most interesting feature of the ruins are the sculptured reliefs which adorn the exterior of the flank walls of the stairs. Each of them is only partly preserved, but the complete group seems to have represented a furious monster pursuing a man, who is flying precipitately before it. The creature, half-brute and half-reptile, is beaked, horned, and winged, with huge protruding eyes. The artist has represented the climax of the struggle, when the monster overtakes his unfortunate victim; its raised paw crushes the left leg of the fleeing man; the terrible beak opens wide and is about to devour his head. The latter in his desperation raises his left arm and thrusts a dagger into the throat of his enemy.

This is the scene as depicted on the left flank wall of the southern staircase. On the right flank wall of the western stair, the monster

---

[1] *Rajat.*, vii, 570.   [2] *Ibid.*, viii, 1529 *et seq.*

and the ornamental wheels behind are much better preserved, though unfortunately the forepart of the relief containing the man is missing. The monster here has a curly mane, an ornamental necklace, and foliated wings. Its rear paw has five toes, four of which—three in front and one behind—are visible. Behind are two highly decorated discs.

PAYAR

Three miles farther, and situated at the foot of the *karewa* on the opposite side of the rivulet, is the village of Payar, which contains a very elegant little temple (Plates LI and LXIII). The name Payach, which has obtained currency through Vigne and Cunningham, is not known locally. The identification of the temple with the temple of Narendrasvami, built by Narendraditya circa A.D. 483-490, proposed by General Cunningham, is in keeping neither with the style of architecture according to which it could be assigned to about the eleventh century A.D. nor with its dedication to Śiva, as the name Narendrasvami would presuppose its dedication to Vishnu.

This temple, in spite of, or perhaps more correctly on account of, the feeble attempt that has been made to dismantle it—the top stone of the roof is still out of position—is by far the best preserved example of a mediæval Kashmiri shrine. It is 8′ square internally and 21′ high, including the base, the chief mouldings of which are a plain torus in the middle and a filleted torus on the top. The sanctum is open on all sides, but is reached only by a single flight of steps on the east side. The doorways are rectangular, and are surmounted by a trefoil arch, which in turn is enclosed by a pediment. The pilasters on which the pediments rest are surmounted by capitals bearing pairs of geese with long foliate tails, and the pilasters from which the trefoiled arch springs are crowned by recumbent bull capitals. The bulls have scarves tied to their humps. The eastern trefoil itself encloses a relief, in which Śiva is seen seated cross-legged on a throne under the canopy of an overhanging tree, surmounted by votaries, two of whom are seated, European fashion, with legs hanging down. On the north side the relief represents Bhairava, the terrible manifestation of Śiva, pursuing a human being, who turns towards him in an attitude of supplication. Behind the Bhairava is a long elephant's trunk. On the west side is the very animated figure of six-armed dancing Śiva. The upper two arms are raised aloft, holding the two ends of a scarf. The middle two hands are gesticulating, the lowest left hand holds a flower and the right the trident, the special emblem of Śiva. In the left lower corner of the group is a musician playing on a *vina* (lute); on the right is another beating a drum in accompaniment.

The southern relief represents a three-headed Śiva seated cross-legged on a wicker-work pedestal. The god is only two-armed and wears the Brahmanical thread. In the left lower corner is a seated female, probably his consort, Parvati. The remaining three figures are emaciated, and are perhaps those of ascetics. Over the god's head is seen the flying figure of a Yakhsha. The corner pilasters are crowned by very beautiful floral capitals.

The roof is pyramidal, and is divided into two sections by an ornamental band, consisting of square spaces alternately projecting and receding. "The latter are occupied by flowers, but the pro-jecting ends are carved into three upright mouldings slightly rounded at the top and surmounted by a straight and horizontal band."[1] The resemblance of these triglyph ornaments to the dentils of classical architecture is remarkably striking. The blank sides of the upper pyramid are relieved by gabled niches which are replicas of the door-ways, the only difference being that the trefoil of the latter is replaced by a semicircular top, and the tympanum is filled by a flower-ornament. The four pediments as well as the apex of the roof were crowned by ribbed melon-like ornaments, two of which are still in existence.

The superstructure is built of ten stones only. "In the interior the walls are plain, but the roof is hollowed out into a hemispherical

[1] *J.A.S.B.*, 1848, part ii, p. 256 *et seq.*

dome of which the centre is decorated by an expanded lotus flower. The lower edge of the dome is ornamented by three straight-edged fillets and by a beaded circle. The spandrels are filled by single undraped and winged figures (of rather spirited execution), who with outstretched arms and legs appear to be supporting the roof. . . . They are probably Yakhshas. The dome itself rests upon the cornice, which is formed of six plain straight-lined mouldings."[1] The ceiling of the Pandrethan temple is a copy of this on a larger scale. The cult image of the temple is a Śiva-linga, which has an octagonal base.

NARASTAN

This is a village situated a little over 20 miles from Avantipur and reached by a rough bridle-path. The road branches off from the Avantipur-Tral road and, skirting the barren hills on the left, debouches into the Arpal valley. From Arpal village Narastan is only 6 miles distant.

The temple (Plate LII), with the exception of the roof, is very well preserved, and possesses several interesting features. It is built on a single base which, unlike other examples of its kind, consists of only four instead of five courses of stones. The cornice is a plain, straight-lined, filleted course, of which only the topmost fillet is rounded off into a cyma recta moulding. The base is, as usual, square. The corner pilasters project very slightly from the temple walls. In the middle of each wall is a trefoiled recess surmounted by a high-pitched double pediment. This in turn is enclosed by a very shallow closed trefoiled arch, surmounted by a two-storied pediment. The capitals from which the pediments spring are crowned by human-headed birds, facing each other; they are very similar to those of Avantipur. The apex of the pediments is decorated with a squat human figure, which may represent Garuda.

An interesting feature of the temple is the novel treatment of

[1] *J.A.S.B.*, 1848, part ii, pp. 257-58.

the trefoil arches on the exterior of the shrine walls; the lower trefoil arch is usually shallow or closed, but the upper trefoil is deeply recessed.   At Narastan the process has been reversed; the lower trefoil encloses a deeply recessed niche, whereas the upper arch is so shallow that it projects only 2″ from the plain wall surface. Another remarkable feature is the absence of a circumambulatory path on top of the base, which is a universal feature in temple bases of this size in Kashmir.

The shrine is reached from the courtyard by a flight of four steps.   The pilasters of the side-walls of the staircase are adorned with shallow trefoil arches from the apex of which hang two swags of beaded garlands.

The portico projects about 4′ from the temple wall.   Its outer surface is plain except for two pairs of human-headed birds which adorn the capitals.   The inner walls of the pilasters are decorated with two pedimental niches, each of which contains the six-armed figure of a goddess.   The upper two hands hold a pitcher and a full-blown lotus; the middle two were probably crossed over the breast; and the lower two hang downwards, but the objects they hold are too defaced to be identified.   There are miniature fluted columns, standing on bases and surmounted by capitals like those of Avantipur, on each side of the niche.   Underneath them are three similar niches containing atlantes.

Internally the temple cell is 8′ 6″ square.   It faces south and contained a Śiva-linga.   Its walls are quite plain except for a string-course at a height of 7′ 6″ from the floor, which resembles somewhat the cornice of the plinth outside, and a small double-pedimented niche on the east wall, the upper pediment of which is decorated with the carved figure of a kneeling human being.   The left pilaster of the niche is only half-carved, which is another illustration of the method of work of the ancient sculptors who were accustomed to carving large stone blocks *in situ*.   Unlike most of the other temples, this one does not possess a ceiling.   The walls rise perpendicularly

9

until the level of the eaves is reached. From this point they begin to contract. Each course is made to project slightly beyond the one below it, until at last the space became so narrow as to be spanned by one square stone, upon which doubtless was placed a finial.

The courtyard is 70' square. It is surrounded by a wall which is unornamented except for a plain filleted string-course at about 2' from the ground, a pedimental trefoiled niche in the west wall, and a recess 3' square. It is roofed over by a coping of sloping stones which rest on a cornice similar to the string-course below. There is a small side entrance near the south-western angle of the enclosure wall. In front of the temple stairs is a square tank about 8' square and over 2' deep. An elaborate stone conduit poured water into it. The spout of the conduit is carved in front with a full-blown lotus through the centre of which the water flows; its sides are decorated with grinning *makara* heads. Above the spout is a stone platform 12' by 6' 3", which probably served as a bathing place, and in summer would be an admirable place for an afternoon siesta, the more so as the water-conduit runs through its centre. From the tank a drain conducts the water to a chamber in the south-eastern corner of the enclosure wall, whence it makes its final exit from the temple yard. This chamber is 9' 6" by 12' 3", and is entered through a narrow doorway 5' 8" by 1' 6". It has a small trefoiled pedimented window 1' 3" by 1' pierced in the wall at a height of 3' 1" above the ground. It probably served as the bathroom of female worshippers.

Only a few feet to the north of this chamber is a small shrine 2' 10" square internally. It has a sloping roof and its ceiling was of superimposed squares like that of the Pandrethan temple.

Exactly opposite the sanctum in the middle of the south wall is the gateway. It consists as usual of a double chamber, each measuring 7' by 4', connected by a doorway. Each of the chambers was faced by a pair of half-engaged round columns. The lintel of the doorway was, on the outside, carved with a row of crenellations alternating with squares surmounted by lozenges.

The temple is built of greyish limestone and was originally covered with a thick coat of lime plaster, traces of which still exist.

MARTAND

The temple of Martand (Plates LIII and LXXIII) is situated at a distance of 5 miles from the town of Anantnag. Being on the top of a lofty plateau, at whose feet stretch the broad verdant plains of Kashmir intersected by a network of rivers, lakes, and canals, thickly dotted with clusters of busy villages nestling like beehives in closely planted groves of trees, and encircled by snow-clad mountain ramparts—the temple of the Sun, as Martand originally was, commands a superb view, such as the eye rarely lights upon. It is this beauty of situation that contributes so largely to the sense of grandeur with which the sight of these ruins always inspires even the most unimaginative visitors.

Like most mediæval temples of Kashmir, Martand consists of a courtyard with the principal shrine in the middle and a colonnaded peristyle. The latter is 220′ long by 142′ broad and contains eighty-four fluted columns facing the courtyard. The peristyle is externally plain, except on the west side, which originally had a row of columns similar to that of the Avantipur temples.

" The entrance, or gateway, stands in the middle of the western side of the quadrangle, and is of the same width as the temple itself. This proportion is in accordance with the ideas of Hindu architectural grandeur; for the rules laid down by them, as quoted by Ram Raz, give different proportions from six-sevenths to ten-elevenths of the width of the temple, for each different style of gateway from the most simple to the most magnificent. Outwardly the Martand gateway resembles the temple itself in the disposition of its parts and in the decoration of its pediments and pilasters. It was open to west and east, and was divided into distinct portions forming an inner and outer portico, by a cross wall with a doorway in the centre, which was no doubt closed with a wooden door. On each flank of the gateway the pediment was supported by massive fluted pillars, 17½′ in height,

or 8′ higher than those in the quadrangle.   One of these is still standing to the south of the entrance; and the style of the architrave and
entablature which connected these pillars with the gateway must have
been the same as that of the architrave in the Avantisvami temple
described above.   I surmise that the front and back pediments of the
gateway were supported on similar large pillars; but it is possible that
the square foundations, which I observed in the front, may have been
only the remains of the wing-walls of a flight of steps.   The roof was
no doubt pyramidal; for a portion of the sloping mouldings of its pediment was still to be seen on one side."[1]   The walls of the gateway
are profusely decorated internally and externally, the chief motif of
decoration being rows of double pedimented niches alternating with
rectangular panels.   Most of the pedimented niches contained single
standing figures of gods; occasionally they also contained an amorous
group similar to those at Avantipur.   The rectangular panels contained sitting groups, floral scrolls, pairs of geese, etc.   Each of the
two large niches in the side-walls of the inner chamber of the gateway
contains the tall figure of a three-headed Vishnu standing between two
attendants.   Immediately below is the long rectangular panel decorated with a row of dancing urchins striking a variety of attitudes.
The temple proper " is 63′ in length by 36′ in width at the eastern
end and only 27′ in width at the western or entrance end.   It contains three distinct chambers, of which the outermost, named *ar-
dhamandapa* or ' half temple,' answering to the front porch of classical
fanes, is 18′ 10″ square; the middle one, called *antarala* or ' mid
temple,' corresponding to the pronaos of the Greeks, is 18′ by 4½′; and
the innermost, named *garbhagriha*, or ' womb of the edifice,' the
naos of the Greeks and the cella of the Romans, is 18′ 5″ by 13′ 10″.
The first is open and highly decorated in accordance with its name,
mandapa, meaning literally ' ornamented.'   The middle chamber is
decorated in the same style; but the inner chamber is plain and is
closed on three sides.   The walls of the temple itself are 9′ thick and

[1] *J.A.S.B.*, 1848, part ii, pp. 269-70.

of its entrance chamber only 4½' thick, being respectively one half and one fourth of the interior width of the building."[1]

" Among the images carved on the walls of the *antarala* and the antechamber, we notice on the left wall of the former a well executed image of the river-goddess Ganga, standing upon her vehicle, the crocodile, which is looking up towards her. A female attendant on her right holds an umbrella over her head, and a *chaurī*-bearer is on her left. She holds her usual emblems, a water pot in her left hand and the stalk of a lotus flower in her right. (She is crowned with a double conical tiara.) On the opposite side of the *antarala* is the river-goddess Yamuna, with her vehicle, the tortoise. Above the niche in the north wall is a relief consisting of a pair of Gandharvas in flight with an umbrella over them.[2] The statues on the western walls of the antechamber are undoubtedly representations of Vishnu, and what Mr. Fergusson mistook for hoods of snakes are in reality points of their coronets. Each of them is three-faced, like the Vishnu image found in the Avantisvami temple, the left face being that of a boar (Varaha) and the right one that of a man-lion (Narasimha). Both are eight-armed, and their lower hands are placed on the heads of *chaurī*-bearers, as in other images of Vishnu found in the valley. Furthermore, they wear the garland (*vanamālā*) and we also notice the bust of the earth-goddess (Prithivi) between the feet of the statue on the north wall. Most of the hands of the images are unfortunately broken and weather-worn, and the emblems they hold can no longer be identified. Nor can the fourteen seated figures which occur on the walls of the antechamber below the cornice be identified with certainty. Twelve of them occur in the north and south walls—*i.e.*, six on each, and two on the east wall. Of the two panels on the east wall, the one on the right seems to represent Aruna, the charioteer of Surya, holding the reins of his seven horses. The pilasters of the great trefoil arch of the

[1] *Op. cit.*, pp. 263-64.
[2] The flying figures are more probably those of Yakshas holding a three-peaked crown which is surmounted by the umbrella.

antechamber contain images which cannot yet be identified."[1]   " The chapels to the north and south of the antechamber each contain two niches 5' 9" by 4' internally, which face to the east and west respectively, possibly an allusion to the rising and setting of the sun."[2]

The roof seems to have been of the pyramidal type common in the temples of Kashmir.

" Such was once the magnificent mass of building dedicated to the worship of the Sun, a mass 75' in height, 33' in length, and the same in width including the wings.   Entrance was gained by a wide flight of steps which are now covered by ruins.   On each of the other sides was a closed doorway surmounted by a trefoiled arch, and covered by a pediment which rose to a height of 60'.   At the angles of the buildings on each side of the doorway were stout pilasters, which were divided into panels, each decorated with a miniature representation of the Aryan style of temple.   These pilasters sustained the entablature, and gave a look of strength and solidity to the walls which was fully needed for the support of the vast and massive roof.   This lofty pyramid of stone was itself rendered lighter and more elegant in appearance by being broken into two portions separated by an ornamental band, and by the addition of small niches with pointed roofs and trefoiled recesses, all of which were in strict keeping with the general character of the building."[3]

The peristyle is the largest example of its kind in Kashmir.   In the middle of its larger sides there are a pair of large fluted pillars, 13' in height and $8\frac{3}{4}'$ apart, somewhat advanced beyond the line of the other cells.   " The quadrangle itself contained seventy round, fluted pillars, and ten square parallel pillars which with the four pillars of the central porches make up the number of 84, that was sacred to the sun.   Of these about one-half, all more or less imperfect, now remain standing. . . .   Each pillar was $9\frac{1}{2}'$ in height, and $21\frac{1}{2}"$ in diameter, with an intercolumniation of 6' $9\frac{1}{2}"$. . . .   The imposts (behind)

[1] *A.S.R.*, 1915-16, pp. 62-63.   [2] *Op. cit.*, p. 63.

[3] *J.A.S.B.*, 1848, part ii, p. 266.

were surmounted by human-headed birds facing each other, and a smaller bird, looking to the front, ornamented the horizontal mouldings of the pediments. . . .

" About one-third of this entablature still exists, principally on the north-eastern side of the quadrangle.

" The other walls of the quadrangle are ornamented by a succession of trefoil-headed panels similar in shape and size to the recessed openings of the interior."[1]   As suggested above, it is probable that its western outer façade was adorned by a series of columns similar to that of the two temples at Avantipur.

There is some uncertainty regarding the exact ascription of this temple, owing to the ambiguity of Kalhana's statement.   But the most probable assumption, which is strengthened by the architectural style, is that the temple as it exists today was built by King Lalitaditya in the middle of the eighth century A.D.

The courtyard of the temple was excavated recently, and a vast quantity of debris and stones was removed.   Among other movable antiquities which the excavations yielded, the most noteworthy are a number of large earthen jars which were found embedded in the floor of the courtyard.   Removal of the accumulated debris of centuries from the base of the temple has also brought to light a very important fact—viz., that previous to the construction of the present temple there existed another temple of somewhat smaller dimensions at this site.   When the new temple was built, the older temple base was not demolished, but was enveloped by a new base of larger dimensions, as is borne out by the existence of both bases, side by side, one *within* the other, on the east side of the temple.   The older temple was probably the one built on this site by Ranaditya.

[1] *J.A.S.B.*, 1848, part ii, p. 271 *et seq.*

BUMAZUV CAVE AND TEMPLES

The little village of Bumazuv is situated only a mile to the north of the sacred springs of Bavan (Matan). It contains the only important group of artificial caves in Kashmir. They are very unpretentious excavations and only one of them possesses architectural interest. It is carved out of a large mass of limestone cliffs overlooking a scene of great beauty, comprising the whole of the lower section of the Lidar valley. The stone in which this excavation is made is of a very friable nature. The façade of the gateway has, therefore, been built of stone masonry in lime. It consists of a single trefoil-arched doorway, surmounted by a pediment, and side walls. On the left-side wall is a small rectangular niche measuring 2′ 2″ by 1′ 1″. Its pilasters are carved with floral scrolls of extraordinary delicacy. The lintel is ornamented with a row of rosettes and the cornice with a row of slightly projecting dentils, whose intervening spaces appear to have been filled with figures of dancing dwarfs, all of which are now defaced. In its interior is a small temple which is similar in style to other temples of Kashmir. It is 9′ 5″ square externally and stands on a base 4′ 6″ in height. A remarkable feature, which points to its being a decadent example, is the very slight projection of the porch. The corner pilasters have two rectangular niches.

In the village, at the foot of the cave, are two temples which have been converted into Muslim ziarats. Both of them are now covered with a thick coat of mud plaster, under which all the artistic and architectural features are concealed. The larger temple now goes by the name of the Ziarat of Baba Bamdin Sahib, who is said to have been a disciple of Shaikh Nur-ud-din, the famous Muslim saint of Kashmir. The pyramidal roof is buried under a mound of earth which surmounts the modern square double wooden roof. The interior measures 8′ square. The ceiling consists of overlapping stones, like that of the Pandrethan temple. The uppermost stone is carved with a full-blown lotus.   The entrance is in the north wall.   Unless the coat of plaster is removed it is impossible to say whether the temple was open on other sides.

To the west of this temple are the ruins of a smaller temple.   The exterior of the roof is destroyed, but the ceiling inside is intact and is similar to the ceiling of the larger temple.   Its porches are exact replicas of those of the cave temple, a fact which leads to the surmise that all three were built at about the same time.

The larger temple has been identified with the Bhimakeśava[1] shrine built by Bhima Shahi of Gandhara, the maternal grandfather of Queen Didda, who ruled Kashmir as the wife of Kshemagupta from A.D. 950-958, and as sole sovereign from A.D. 980-1003.

Achhabal

The spring of Achhabal is perhaps the largest spring in Kashmir. Its old Hindu name was Akshvala, but it does not seem to have been much known in mediæval times.   Abul Fazl speaks of it in the *Ain-i-Akbari* as " a fountain which shoots up to the height of a cubit, and is scarce equalled for its coldness, limpidity, and refreshing qualities.   The sick that drink of it and persevere in a course of its waters, recover their health."

Bernier, who visited it in A.D. 1665, speaks of its beauties in the following glowing terms:

"Returning from Send-bray,[2] I turned a little from the high road for the sake of visiting Achiavel, a country house formerly of the kings of Kachemire and now of the Great Mogol.   What principally constitutes the beauty of this place is a fountain whose waters disperse themselves into a hundred canals round the house, which is by no means unseemly, and throughout the gardens.   The spring gushes out of the earth with violence, as if it issued from the bottom of some well, and the water is so abundant that it ought rather be called a

---

[1] *Rajat.*, vi., verse 178 note.   [2] *I.e.*, Trisandhya.

river than a fountain. It is excellent water and cold as ice. The garden is very handsome, laid out in regular walks, and full of fruit trees, apple, pear, plum, apricot, and cherry; jets-d'eau in various forms and fish-ponds are in great number; and there is a lofty cascade which in its fall takes the form and colour of a large sheet, thirty or forty paces in length, producing the finest effect imaginable, especially at night, when innumerable lamps, fixed in parts of the wall adapted for that purpose, are lighted under this sheet of water." This description, but for the dilapidated aspect of the tanks and water-courses, the comparative absence of fruit trees, and the total absence of nocturnal illuminations, might very well apply to the Achhabal garden of today. The cart-road and the dak bangalow have en-croached upon its lowest terrace, though the original watercourse is still intact, and the foundations of its row of fountains are still visible in the water. A quaint doorway built in the time of the late Maharaja Ranbir Singhji gives admittance to the second terrace of the garden. Most of the *barahdaris* and pavilions belong to the repairs executed in the reign of the Maharaja Ranbir Singhji. Only the ruins of the pavilion over the fountain itself, standing solitary yet strong in defiance of the rushing waters and of the destructive vegetation, belong to Mughal times. This garden does not possess any sloping cascades. All the falls are vertical. To the west of the garden are, or rather were, the royal quarters, the present buildings being modern and contemporaneous with the pavilions. The hammam of Jahangir, however, is in excellent preservation. The objects specially note-worthy here are a piece of a timber conduit lying in the compound and said to belong to Mughal times, and the system of earthen pipes which conveyed water to the royal bathrooms from the subterranean channel in the uppermost terrace of the garden.

Achhabal is an ideal place for laying out a garden. "Nowhere else have I seen such possibilities for a combined appeal, of a stately stone-bordered pleasance between ordered avenues of full-grown trees, and a natural rock and woodland upper garden with haunting

far-reaching views, where the white wild roses foam over the firs
and the boulders rivalling the sheet of water Bernier praised."[1]

KOTHER

The village of Kother is situated two miles above Achhabal, a
little off the Achhabal-Kashtwar road.   The name is derived from
Kapateśvara, which is a contraction of Papasudana-Kapateśvara, an
appellation of Śiva to whom the spring here is sacred.   The place
has for many centuries past enjoyed a great reputation for sanctity.
King Bhoja of Malva, who was a contemporary of King Ananta
(A.D. 1028-1063) of Kashmir, " had the round tank (*kuṇḍa*) constructed at Kapateśvara with heaps of gold that he sent.   King
Bhoja vowed that he would always wash his face in the water from
the *Papasudana tīrtha*, and this (man Padmaraja) made the fulfil-
ment of his difficult vow (possible) by regularly despatching from this
(*tīrtha*) large numbers of glass jars filled with that water."[2]   The
tank is circular.   The stone basin built by Bhoja is still partially
extant.   The flights of steps flanked by side-walls which are surmounted by the cornices usual in Kashmiri temples, facing north and
south respectively, lead down to the water level.   By the side of the
spring are two small temples which seem to be contemporaneous
with the stone wall of the spring.   The larger temple measures
8′ 4″ internally and faces south-west.   Its roof seems to have been
destroyed by fire.   The entrance is 3′ 8″ by 6′, and it is noteworthy
that the recesses on the exterior of the other three sides, which in
most other temples are of about the same dimensions as the open
doorway, are in this instance much smaller.

The smaller temple measures 6′ 4″ internally.   It faces west.

[1] Mrs. Villiers-Stuart, *Gardens of the Great Mughals*, p. 191.

[2] *Rajat.*, vii, verses 190-93.   It is interesting to note that a large number of ancient
glass fragments are still found strewn on the road which leads to the spring from the
village.   They seem to indicate that the locality had in old times a flourishing glass
industry.

Its lower part is buried underground. There is a long stretch of wall 246′ long and about 12′ wide, on the north side of the area, which originally formed part of the enclosure wall round the temples and the tank. The fragment that is above ground on the east side shows that this surrounding wall is in reality a cellular peristyle. The top stones of the cells are visible.

A curious local legend reports that a treasure lies buried somewhere in or near the spring, and that there was a stone slab embedded in the wall of the spring on which were inscribed directions for its discovery and expenditure on the repairs and upkeep of the spring and its dependent shrines. The same legend associates the name of a king Mutskund with the foundation of the temples. In support of this the people quote the adage:—

> Mutsakund razas manshihandi kan
> Tim kati tsalanas ? Kuther van.

Translation : King Mutsukund has buffalo's ears : where will they be removed ?   In the wood of Kother.

He is said to have been favoured by nature with a pair of buffalo's ears, of which he was anxious to rid himself, but he could not achieve his purpose by any means at his disposal. At length, being advised to try a bath in the waters of this spring, he had his heart's desire. In gratitude he expended his treasures upon the foundation and upkeep of the temples and the spring.

Note.—Since the above was written, the area round the spring has been excavated, and, as was expected, a cellular quadrangle and a number of shrines belonging to the tenth to eleventh centuries have been exhumed. Stratigraphical evidence shows that there was an older stratum of buildings also, upon which the structures of the tenth to eleventh centuries were superimposed.

Mamal

The small temple of Mamal (ancient Mamalaka) is situated on the right bank of the Lidar, exactly opposite the State Rest House at Pahalgam. For one who has seen the great temples of Martand and Avantipur, the journey to Mamal and back for the sole purpose of seeing this temple is perhaps not worth the trouble. But a visitor whom other pursuits call to Pahalgam should not miss seeing it.

The temple is 8′ square internally, and has in front a porch supported on two fluted columns, one of which is missing. The superstructure has fallen down. No remnants of the ceiling are left. The walls are straight and vertical above the string course, and it is probable that originally there was no ceiling, as at Narastan.

It may well be that this temple is the same as that of Mammeśvara, which the *Rajatarangini* mentions King Jayasimha (A.D. 1128-1155) to have adorned with a golden *kalaśa*, or finial. Its architecture also shows certain features which are undoubtedly decadent. One of these is the absence of projection in the corner pilasters. The temple was externally covered with a thick coat of lime plaster. It contains an old pedestal and a probably modern Śiva-linga. A spring of remarkably pure water rises under the site of the temple. Its waters are enclosed in a basin in front of the stairs. The whole was originally surrounded by a rubble-stone wall, of which the foundations are still visible on the north side.

Vernag

The spring of Vernag is the reputed source of the river Vitasta. In Hindu times it was known as the Nila-naga, and was sacred to the snake-deity of that name. The *Nilamata Purana* tells us that when Parvati had obtained the consent of her consort Śiva to incarnate in Kashmir as the river Vitasta in order to purify the country which had been defiled by the touch of Piśachas, who appear to have been some outlandish barbarians, he struck the earth at the site of the spring with his trident, and thus cleared the way for the issue of the waters of the Parvati-Vitasta from the nether world. Hence the *tirtha* also bore the alternative name of *Śulaghata*, " trident stroke." It seems to have retained considerable importance among Hindu places of pilgrimage even as late as Akbar's time, for Abul Fazl[1] mentions the existence, to the east, of a number of stone temples. In his time it had already taken its present name of Vernag, borrowing it probably from the district of Ver, the name at that time of the modern Shahabad Pargana. Abul Fazl adds that " it is a pool measuring a *jarib*, which tosses in foam with an astonishing roar, and its depth is unfathomable, and is surrounded by a stone embankment. . . ."

The construction of the octagonal basin and the arcade (Plate LIV) which now surrounds it, was commenced by Jahangir and completed in the time of Shah Jahan. The former writes:[2] " It is an octagonal reservoir about 20 yards by 20 yards. Near it are the remains of a place of worship for recluses: cells cut out of the rock and numerous caves. The water is exceedingly pure. Although I could not guess its depth, a grain of poppy-seed is visible until it touches the bottom. There are many fish to be seen in it. As I had heard that it was unfathomable, I ordered them to throw in a cord with a stone attached, and when this cord was measured in *gaz* it became evident that the depth was not more than one and a half the height of a man. After my accession I ordered them to build the sides of the spring with stone, and they made a garden round it with a canal; and built halls and houses about it, and made a place such that travellers over the world can point out few like it." This information from the pen of the Emperor himself probably accounts for the complete disappearance of the stone temples and caves, whose materials would

[1] *Ain-i-Akbari*, vol. ii, p. 361.
[2] *Tuzuk-i-Jahangiri* (Oriental Translation Fund), p. 92.

afford the persons in charge of building operations too tempting a quarry to be lightly set aside. Of the buildings which Jahangir ordered to be constructed here only the range of twenty-four arches round the spring remains partially intact. The arches were originally built of stone, the walls being surmounted by a row of beautifully carved brackets which supported the eaves. A number of these are still in existence. On two sides of the octagon are larger chambers, each containing a staircase leading to the upper storey, no trace of which is left. The brick facing of the majority of the arches, as well as ruins of the walls of the second storey over the entrance chamber, belong to the repairs done by Wazir Punnu in the reign of the late Maharaja Ranbir Singhji. Two inscribed stone tablets, one belonging to the time of Jahangir and the other to that of Shah Jahan, are built into the wall of the arcade. The inscription of Shah Jahan was originally fixed in the wall of the entrance chamber, but was for some unknown reason removed some years ago by the Public Works Department contractor who was commissioned to raise the floor of the promenade round the spring, presumably for irrigation purposes. The raising of the level of the promenade accounts for the markedly stunted appearance of the arcade. Jahangir's inscription, which is dated the fifth year of his reign, runs as follows:—

Padshah-i haft-kishwar 'adalat-gustar 'abu-al muzaffar Nurud Din Jahangir ibn
    Akbar Shah Ghazi batarikh-i
Sanah 5 julus darin Sar-chashma faiz-amin nazul ajlal farmudand; tarikh:—
Az Jahangir Shah-i Akbar Shah
In bina sar kashidah bar aflak
Bani-e aqal yaft tarikhash
Qasr abad-o chashma-i Varnag.

Translation: The king of the seven dominions, the Dispenser of Justice, the Victorious Lord, Nur-ud-Din Jahangir, son of Akbar Shah Ghazi, bestowed grace upon this bounteous spring (by his presence) in the fifth year of his reign : the date : . . . .
Through Jahangir Shah, the son of Akbar Shah, this foundation raised its head to the high heavens. The source of wisdom (*i.e.*, the author) discovered its date: May the palace and the spring of Varnag endure (for ever).

The last line gives the date A.H. 1029=A.D. 1619-20.   Shah Jahan's inscription reads thus:—

> Haidar ba hukm-i Shah-i Jahan padshahi dahr
> Shukr-e khuda ki sakht chunin abshar jui
> In jui dada ast zi ju-e bahisht yad
> Zin abshar yafta Kashmir abrui
> Tarikh-i jui guft ba gosham sarosh-i ghaib
> Az chashma-i bihisht birun amadast jui.

Translation : The Lord be praised for that Haidar, by the order of Shah-i Jahan, the monarch of the universe, constructed such a cascade and such a water-course.   This water-course is reminiscent of the stream that flows in heaven ; and the cascade (is such) that (even) Kashmir derives honour from it.   The invisible angel whispered the date (of construction) of the water-course in my ear.   " This stream has sprung from the fountain of heaven."

The last line gives the date A.H. 1036, corresponding to A.D. 1626-27.

After the decline of the Mughal Empire the Hindus reclaimed what they had lost.   Some of the cells are now used as idol chambers, and priests serve as guides to visitors.

The surplus water of the spring was discharged by an underground conduit, the mouth of which is visible from above.   Passing under the buildings the conduit crossed the garden and carried the water to the royal bathrooms, the ruins of which and of other buildings are still to be seen outside the rubble wall on the east side.   The stream which flows from the spring is about 12' in width and runs throughout the length of the garden.   It is spanned in the middle and at the northern end by two modern *barahdaris*.   Only the upper terrace is enclosed, though the presence of the ruined water-chute, over which the stream rushes down, before leaving the garden, suggests the existence of a lower terrace.

The garden, in spite of its much curtailed dimensions, the presence of unsightly huts built by the local priests, and the general dilapidated condition of its streams and buildings, has a distinct charm, of which its royal founder seems to have been quite sensible; for the way-worn

Jahangir, who expired at Chingas near Rajauri on his return journey from Kashmir, prayed with his dying breath to be conveyed to Vernag to be buried there.   The garden with its shady trees, icy-cold water, and murmuring streams, overshadowed by the sombre pine-clad hills, is a place pre-eminently fitted to be the retreat of a recluse and the final resting-place of a world-weary emperor.

VI

MONUMENTS BELOW SRINAGAR

ROUTES

From.	To.	Distance.	Remarks.
Srinagar	Parihasapura	14 miles by the Baramula cart road, and 3 miles on foot or pony beyond	
Srinagar	Patan	17 miles	Rest house
Patan	Baramula and Ushkar	17 miles	at Patan
Baramula	Fath Garh	3 miles over the hill	
Baramula	Naranthal	3½ miles on pony	
Baramula	Buniar	14 miles ⎫	Dak at
Buniar	Bandi temple	9 miles ⎭	Rampur
Srinagar	Manasbal	18 miles by motorable road ; or by boat	
Srinagar	Wangath	33 miles—18 miles by motorable road as far as Wayil, thence bridle path	

PARIHASAPURA

The *karewas* of Paraspor and Divar are situated at a distance of fourteen miles from Srinagar on the Baramula road. They were chosen by King Lalitaditya (*c.* A.D. 750) for the erection of a new capital city, and it is certain that, given a sufficient supply of drinking water, the high and dry plateaus of Parihasapura have every advantage over the low, swampy Srinagar as a building site. Lalitaditya and his ministers seem to have vied with each other in embellishing the new city with magnificent edifices which were intended to be worthy alike of the king's glory and the ministers' affluence. The plateau is studded with heaps of ruins of which a few have been excavated. Among these the most important are three Buddhist structures, a stupa, a monastery, and a *chaitya*. Their common features are the enormous size of the blocks of limestone used in their construction, the smoothness of their dressing, and the fineness of their joints. The immense pile at the north-eastern corner of the plateau is the stupa (Plate LV.) of Chankuna, the Turkoman (?) minister of Lalitaditya. Its superstructure has entirely disappeared, leaving behind a huge mass of scorched boulders which completely cover the top of the base. There is a large massive block in the middle of this debris, which has a circular hole in the middle, $5'$ deep. It is probable that this stone belonged to the *hti* (finial) of the stupa, and that the hole is the mortice in which was embedded the lower end of the staff of the stone umbrellas which crowned the drum.

The base is $128'$ $2''$ square in plan, with offsets and a flight of steps on each side. Its mouldings are of the usual type, a round torus in the middle and a filleted torus as the cornice. The steps were flanked by plain rails and side walls which had pilasters in front decorated with carved figures of seated and standing atlantes. Some of these are in position, while others, which were lying about loose, have been transported to the Srinagar Museum. They are not grotesque creatures like those so commonly seen in Gandhara, but have the appearance of ordinary respectable gentlemen, whose placid features seem to indicate that the superincumbent weight sits lightly upon them. The top surface of each of the two plinths is broad and affords adequate space for circumambulation. Among the loose architectural stones lying scattered about the site are a few curious blocks in the south-eastern and south-western corners. They are round torus stones adorned with four slanting bands or fillets running round the body. As this type of torus moulding is not used in either of the bases, it is probable that it belonged to the string-course on the drum of the stupa. There are fragments of trefoiled arches also, which contained images of the Buddha and Bodhisattvas.

The large square structure to the south of the stupa is the *rajavihara*, or royal monastery. A flight of steps in the east wall gives access to one of its cells which served as a verandah. The monastery is a quadrangle of twenty-six cells enclosing a square courtyard which was originally paved with stone flags, some of which are extant. In front of the cells was a broad verandah, which was probably covered, the roof being supported by a colonnade which ran along the edge of the plinth. A flight of steps corresponding to the one mentioned above leads down to the courtyard. Exactly opposite to this, in the middle of the west wall, are three cells preceded by a vestibule, which is built on a plinth projected into the courtyard. It is probable that these were the apartments occupied by the abbot of the monastery. Near a corner of it is a large stone trough, which may have served as a water reservoir for bathing purposes. A couple of stone drains passing underneath cells Nos. 18 and 21 (if we begin counting from the cell to the south of the entrance chamber) carry off the rain and other surplus water from the courtyard. Externally the plinth is about 10' high. In cell No. 25 (that is the one to the north of the entrance chamber) was found a small earthen jug which contained forty-four silver coins in excellent preservation. They belonged to the time of kings Vinayaditya, Vigraha, and Durlabha. They are now exhibited in the Numismatic Section of the Srinagar Museum. The monastery was repaired at a subsequent period. The repairs are plainly distinguishable in the exterior of the wall on the eastern and western sides.

The building next to it on the south side is the *chaitya* built by Lalitaditya. It stands on a double base of the usual type. A flight of steps on the east side leads to the entrance, which must originally have been covered by a large trefoil-arch, fragments of which are lying about the site. This building possesses some of the most massive blocks of stone that have ever been used in Kashmiri temples, and which compare favourably with those used in ancient Egyptian buildings. The floor of the sanctum is a single block 14' by 12' 6" by 5' 2".

The sanctum is 27' square surrounded by a circumambulatory

passage. It is probable that its ceiling was supported on four columns, the bases only of which survive at the four corners. The roof, which was probably supported on the massive stone walls of the *pradakshina*, may have been of the pyramidal type.

The courtyard is enclosed by a rubble-stone wall which has nothing remarkable about it. In front of the temple steps is the base of a column which probably supported the *dhvaja*, or banner, bearing the special emblem of the deity enshrined in the sanctuary.

The flank walls of the stair were adorned with atlantes similar to those of the stupa.

Near the *chaitya* is the foundation of a small building of the diaper-rubble style.

While this plateau was reserved for the erection of Buddhist buildings only, the other two were exclusively appropriated by Hindus. Perhaps the arrangement was intentional, to avoid possible friction between the two powerful religious bodies. On the *karewa* locally known as Gordan there are ruins of a Hindu temple which are probably all that remain of Lalitaditya's temple of Govardhanadhara. Crossing the ravine in which nestles the little village of Diwar-Yakmanpura, and ascending the plateau opposite, are seen the immense ruins of two extraordinarily large temples—one of them has a peristyle larger than that of Martand — which may represent Lalitaditya's favourite shrines of Parihasakesava and Muktakesava.

PATAN

Sugandhesa Temple

The *Rajatarangini* mentions the erection of three temples at Patan, which in ancient days was called Śankarapurapattana, after the name of its founder, King Śankaravarman (A.D. 883-902). Perhaps it would be well to remark here that vandalism of a serious kind had already begun in pre-Muslim times, as some of the materials used in the construction of these temples were removed from the older site of Parihasapura described above. The three temples named by the Kashmir chronicle are (1) Śankaragauriśvara, (2) Sugandheśa, and (3) Ratnavardhaneśa. The first, identified with the larger temple near Patan, was built by the king himself, the second, which is the one nearer Srinagar, is named after Sugandha, his queen, and the third, of which no trace has so far been found, if we exclude the architectural fragments near the spring outside the dak bangalow, was built by Ratnavardhana, his minister. All three were dedicated to Śiva.

The Sugandheśa temple does not differ materially from other temples of Kashmir. The shrine is 12′ 7″ square and has, as usual, a portico in front. It is open on one side only, and has trefoiled niches externally on the other sides. These niches contained images. The temple stands on a double base, but it seems probable from the flank walls of the lower stair and the frieze of the lower base, in which the panels intended for sculpture decoration have been merely blocked out, but not carved, that the temple was never completed.

The entrance to the courtyard is in the middle of the eastern wall of the peristyle, and consists, as usual, of two chambers with a partition wall and a doorway in the middle.

Among the architectural fragments lying loose on the site, the most noteworthy are (a) two fragments of fluted columns with their capitals, (b) two bracket capitals with voluted ends and carved figures of atlantes supporting the frieze above, (c) a huge stone belonging to the cornice of the temple, bearing rows of kirtimukhas (grinning lions' heads) and rosettes, and (d) a stone probably belonging to the partition wall of the entrance, having (1) two small trefoiled niches in which stand female figures wearing long garlands and (2) below them two rectangular niches, in one of which is an atlant seated between two lions facing the spectator, and in the other are two human-headed birds.

The cornice of the base of the peristyle is similar to that of the

Avantisvami temple.   The cells were preceded by a row of fluted columns, bases of some of which are *in situ* while those of others are scattered about in the courtyard.

The attention of the visitor is called to the slots in the lower stones of the jambs of the cells.   These are mortices for iron clamps which held pairs of stones together.   Pieces of much-corroded iron are still extant in some of the mortices.

Śankaragauriśvara Temple

Lower down is the larger temple built by the king himself (Plate LVI).   It is only an enlarged copy of the queen's temple.   On account of the lack of proper facilities for drainage of rain water it has not been deemed advisable to excavate its courtyard.   The peristyle, the temple-plinth, and a smaller shrine in the north-east corner, are therefore still underground.   The rectangular path around the temple marks the position of the peristyle, tops of some columns of which are seen peeping out of the earth in the south-west corner.   The square flower-bed with a projection on one side in the north-east corner of the courtyard coincides with the small shrine below.   The square space in the middle of the eastern path marks the position of the entrance.

The temple itself is an imposing pile, though a great deal of its grandeur has been taken away by the concealment of its plinth.   The cella is 17' square and the central stone of the floor measures 12' 6" by 10'.   It has nine circular holes arranged in three rows.   It is possible that these were mortices of tenons which held in position the pedestal of the idol.   The left wall of the portico has a trefoiled niche which is divided into two panels.   The lower and larger one contains a number of figures, of which the principal seems to be Śiva.   Above it, in the upper foil, is the squatting figure of the elephant-headed god, Ganeśa, whose presence here would conclusively prove, even if there were any doubt about it, that the temple was dedicated to Śiva.   The jambs of the recesses on the exterior of the temple have half-engaged columns which are decorated with well-executed geometrical and other patterns.   Their capitals are surmounted by human-headed birds.

A few yards to the north of the Patan dak bangalow has recently been excavated an old *baoli* whose waters are confined in three rectangular reservoirs which are connected with each other.   The one in the middle contains a miniature temple constructed originally of three stones (Plate LVII).   The top-stone is missing.   It is 2′ 8″ square externally and is open on all four sides.   The openings seem to have been closed originally with wooden doors.   These little shrines belong to the time when the prosperity of the Hindus had waned, and they were not capable of devoting so much wealth to the glorification of their religion.

Ushkar and Baramula

The village of Ushkar or Wushkur is situated at a distance of half a mile from the Baramula dak bangalow.   The name is a corruption of Huvishkapura, which, according to Kalhana, was the name of a city founded by Huvishka, the great Kushan king in the second century A.D.   It was a flourishing town in mediæval times owing to its position on the principal trade-route between Kashmir and north-western India.   Lalitaditya built here a shrine of Vishnu named *Muktasvamin* and a large vihara with a stupa.[1]   Hsüan-tsang, the famous Chinese pilgrim who visited Kashmir in A.D. 631, entered the valley by the Baramula pass, and spent his first night at one of the monasteries here.   The reigning king accorded him a very hospitable welcome, sending his own mother and younger brother with chariots and horses to escort him to the capital.

Of the monasteries and temples which Hsüan-tsang saw, and Kalhana mentions, none now remain above ground, except the ruins of a stupa and its surrounding wall, a few yards to the west of the village.   On the analogy of style which is similar to that of the great stupa at Parihasapura, there can be little doubt that it is the same structure which the Kashmir chronicle states Lalitaditya built in the

---

[1] *Rajat.*, iv, 188.

middle of the eighth century A.D.   Only the lowest courses of its base are now in position.

An interesting fact about this stupa is that it seems to have been built over an older structure of nearly the same type, stones of which were found *in situ* when the silt round the base was removed some years ago.   That structure may have belonged to Kushan times.   This surmise is strengthened by the discovery outside the north-eastern corner of the surrounding wall, of eleven terracotta heads, besides a number of fragmentary limbs of images which display the unmistakable influence of the Gandhara school of the third and fourth century.   These are now preserved in the Srinagar Museum.

Plate LVIII. (a) illustrates the head of a Bodhisattva.   The unusually ornamental treatment of the hair in this fragment is noteworthy.   The delicate features, rounded chin, and twisted, dandified locks secured by a beaded fillet placed sideways, make the face attractive in spite of the somewhat weary smile and the self-satisfied expression of the face.

(b): The shaggy beard, close-pressed lips, knitted eyebrows, and furrowed forehead, of this Brahman ascetic are so remarkably realistic that it would be difficult to imagine that the artist was not drawing a portrait from life.   The hair is neatly brushed upwards and was probably gathered in a knot at the back of the head, where it was kept in position by an ornamental band.   The ardent gaze and the prominent cheekbones are indicative of self-mortification.

(c): This is one of the most beautiful heads found at Ushkar. The oval face, small nose, sensitive nostrils, soft delicate lips, plump rounded chin, hair smoothly combed back and falling in curly tresses on the shoulders, are all essentially feminine.   She is an *upasika*, or female lay devotee.   Her soft and wistful gaze, intensified by the upturned poise of the face, shows with what a feeling of devotion these feminine worshippers approached the Master.

(d): This illustration represents the head of a contemplative young monk with shaven crown, high forehead, arched eyebrows, and large dreamy eyes.   The remarkably high and narrow skull seems to be the result of lateral pressure, a practice which was once prevalent among certain tribes in Central Asia.[1]

One of the large blocks of stones lying loose in the trench to the north of the stupa bears the Śarada letters *he-sh-ka-ra* incised upon its rough surface, a circumstance which proves that even in Lalita-ditya's time the town was known by its colloquial name, though the dignified Sanskrit original remained in vogue in literature.

Not the least interesting object here is the compact surrounding wall built of extremely small chips of stone in mud.   The entrance to the courtyard must have been on the east side, opposite to the stairs of the stupa.   The lower portion of the wall is extraordinarily thick and served, no doubt, as plinth for a range of cells which ran along its entire length, the upper portion being utilised as their back wall.   The foundations of the wall are pierced at intervals with openings for drains.

Other objects of interest near by are two colossal Śiva-lingas erected at the two ends of the village.

The town of Baramula, properly Varahamula, named after the Boar incarnation of Vishnu, was an important place in mediæval times. The temple of Adi-Varaha, " Primeval Boar," destroyed by Sikandar But-shikan, is said to have been one of the most splendid in Kashmir. Its site is identified, on the strength of local tradition, with the Koti-tirtha situated half a mile below the bridge.   A few architectural stones may still be seen lying about at this place.   The only object of interest which it now contains is the large human-faced Śiva-linga (Plate LIX).

Further down is the site of the old watch-station, known as Drang, which name it has retained from very early times.   It served the double purpose of a customs post and frontier outpost where traffic could be controlled and all suspicious characters apprehended.

---

[1] The description of the sculptures given above is taken from the author's Handbook of the Archæological and Numismatic Sections of the Sri Pratap Museum, Srinagar.

FATHGARH

This is the name of the small village near the mouth of the Narvav valley. It is situated at a distance of nearly three miles from Baramula. It contains the ruins of a very large temple which presents several points of interest. Internally it is 28' 9" square. The greater part of the cella was occupied by a massive platform on which was placed a colossal Śiva-linga, a large fragment of which is lying there still. The platform was decorated with a torus moulding and the space around it was no doubt used as a *pradakshina*. Two fragments of the waterspout (*pranali*), which carried off the washings of the image, are also lying in the sanctum. The front elevation of the platform is decorated with two rows of trefoiled niches, which were probably intended to contain lamps during the evening worship. A point of special interest about this temple is the arrangement of the ceiling. In other temples, as has been remarked above, the ceiling is either composed of overlapping stones which gradually lessen the span until it is sufficiently short to be covered by a single slab, usually circular, or it is straight-lined and triangular in section as at Narastan and Naranthal. Here both these arrangements have been discarded in favour of an elaborate system of corbelling.

A late memorial stele displaying very poor artistic skill has been discovered in the excavation of the cella. The lower panel contains a pair of clumsy human figures seated on stools facing each other. The upper one contains a trident.

The dado of the portico is adorned with a row of pedimented niches.

The open doorway faces north-west and, like the closed recesses on the exterior of the other three sides, was covered by a large trefoiled arch surmounted by a pediment. Its pilasters are, as usual, adorned with half-engaged fluted columns. This temple has a particularly massive appearance and its thorough excavation is very desirable. In the south-east corner of the area is a late brick well.

NARANTHAL

This is the name of a village about two and a half miles below Baramula on the right bank of the river. On the old road to Muzaffarabad and situated at a short distance from the village is a small shrine which is said to have stood in a tank, though today it is on dry ground and no traces of a tank are visible. But there is a spring near by. Only the superstructure of the temple is above ground. It is built of plain blocks of slate which are now very much the worse for wear. There is only one arched entrance on the east side. Traces of a stone floor are visible inside. The second course from the top is formed of a single slab $4\frac{1}{2}'$ square by $1\frac{1}{2}'$ thick.

The interior is a square of $7\frac{1}{4}'$ and is $9'\ 5''$ high. There is no ceiling.

The topmost stone of the roof has a circular mortice in the centre which was originally intended to hold the finial which crowned the apex of the pyramid. The temple is probably of the late mediæval era, not earlier than the twelfth century A.D., and perhaps much later.

BUNIAR

The temple of Buniar (Plates LX and LXXV) is situated on the Jhelum Valley road, two miles above Rampur. It is by far the best preserved of all the larger Kashmir temples.

The gateway is a double-chambered structure faced on each open side by a trefoil arch surmounted by a steep pediment. The lintels of the closed arches are supported on pairs of columns which were originally fluted, though the weather has now left no trace of flutes. They have a double capital, the upper one being voluted on all four sides. The walls are externally surmounted by a cornice of *kirtimukhas*, alternating with miniature trefoiled niches. Upon this rests the first course of the pyramidal roof.

The flights of steps on the eastern and western sides respectively afford entrance to and exit from the entrance chamber. The one on

the roadside is buried underground, but the inner stair has been excavated.   It consists of seven steps flanked by sloping rails and upright side walls.   Between this stair and the temple is a small stone
platform which formed the lowermost course of the stepped base of a
column (most probably a Garudadhvaja).

The priest in charge of the temple has now placed in it a small
stele of very crude workmanship and late date, which he has painted
with vermilion.   Another similar stele, still standing in the position
in which it was found, is seen in front of the temple stair.

The temple itself stands on a double base, which is in every
respect similar to other structures of its kind in Kashmir.
(Plate LXXIV).   A lofty trefoil arch, standing upon advanced
pilasters and enclosing a rectangular entrance originally surmounted
by an ornamental trefoil and steep pediment, gives access to the
sanctum.   The jambs of the entrance are adorned with half-engaged
columns.   The interior is a square of 14 feet.   The pedestal of the
image is placed on a broad platform.   The original image, which
seems to have been of Vishnu, is now replaced by small Śiva-lingas
originally brought from the bed of the river Narbada.   The walls
are covered with a coat of modern whitewash.   The string course
from which the ceiling springs is still visible, but the ceiling itself
which Bishop Cowie saw in 1865 and described as domical, has since
either fallen down or been removed.   It was, no doubt, similar to the
ceilings of the larger temples at Wangath (see page 165 *sq.*, below).

Externally the only decorations are the trefoils of the recesses,
their pediments, and the cornice of *kirtimukhas* and miniature trefoils
from which the roof sprang.

The quadrangle measures 145′ by 119½′, and consists of fifty-
three cells and the gateway.   They are rectangular, 7′ long by 4′
broad.   Each cell has a single trefoiled entrance enclosed in a high-
pitched pediment resting on half-engaged columns.   These ranges
of cells are preceded by a noble colonnade which stands on a base
similar to that of the temple.   A transverse beam connects the

capitals of the columns with the roof of the cells.   Over these beams rises the entablature, only one course of which, namely the frieze of miniature trefoils, is extant (Plate LXXVI).

In the centre of each range of cells, except, perhaps, the one in which the gateway stands, is an apartment of larger dimensions preceded by a pair of taller columns which are advanced about 4' from the rest of the peristyle.

The top course of the cells is also decorated in the same way as the frieze above.

On the south side, projecting from the cornice of the upper base of the temple, is the spout of the channel which carried off the washings of the image.   It seems to have been shaped originally into a *makara*, or crocodile's head.   Immediately below it is a huge water trough carved out of a single block of stone.

The rain-water in the courtyard is carried off by a drain which runs under the south-eastern corner of the peristyle.

In cell No. 11 of the north range, beginning the reckoning from the corner nearest the gateway, is the side entrance, which was then, as now, closed with a wooden door.   The monotony of the external face of the western wall is partially relieved by rows of small square projections.   In its two corners are two cells opening outwards.

Immediately outside the side-door mentioned above is a square structure built of plain blocks of stone.   The middle portion of each of its four walls has fallen down, and the gaps have been filled in with small chips of stone built in mud.   It is difficult to surmise what was its original purpose.

DHATHAMANDIR, OR THE BANDI TEMPLE

The temple known as Dhathamandir is situated on the Jhelum Valley cart road, midway between Rampur and Uri, about two miles below Mohora.   The name signifies " ruined temple."

The only material difference in style between this temple and the one at Buniar is that it does not possess any colonnade, and that the cells, which in the former are built of granite as the temple itself, are here built of *kanjur*, their plinth only being of lime-stone. The jambs of the cells were decorated with half-engaged columns, remnants of which may still be seen in the south-western corner of the peristyle.

The central shrine faces north-east, and is built of a very beautiful green limestone, which, curiously enough, seems to have been covered with a thick coat of lime plaster, decayed fragments of which are still clinging to various parts of the walls. The pedestal of the image is extant. There are two small shrines, replicas of the main building in the north-western corner of the courtyard.

The bases of the columns which supported the trefoil arch of the gateway are still *in situ*. Fragments of columns as well as their beautifully carved capitals are lying about in the compound and the area outside the gateway.

On the hillside, a few yards to the south-east of the temple, are remains of two smaller shrines which, like the subsidiary temples in the courtyard, are replicas of the main temple.

FIROZPOR = DRANG

Firozpor=drang is a small village situated at a distance of a mile and a half from Tang Marg, at the spot where the Firozpor-nala issues from the mountains into the open ground. The latter part of the name preserves the memory of its ancient appellation Karkota-dranga. The term "dranga" was used in pre-Muslim times to indicate a frontier watch-station, established for the purpose of collecting customs duties and of generally safeguarding the frontier. Karkota-dranga (modern Firozpor) controlled the Tosamaidan route to Punch (ancient Parnotsa; Kashmiri Prun<u>ts</u>).

The village contains the ruins of a small temple which was probably originally surrounded by a peristyle, no part of which, except the double-chambered gateway, is now extant above ground. The chief cause of the ruin of this temple seems to have been the unchecked growth of vegetation. Several walnut trees have taken root in the masonry, and are continuing the process of destruction.

The temple faces north-east. The roof has fallen in, and has filled the whole cella with large boulders which have completely hidden the floor, and consequently made it impossible to ascertain to which particular god the shrine was dedicated. Internally it is 11' square. The ceiling seems to have been of the Narastan type. The portico was surmounted by a trefoil-arch and a pediment of the usual type.

Externally also this temple is similar to the Narastan temple, inasmuch as the corner pilasters have very slight projection and the trefoiled recesses on the sides are smaller than the arch of the portico. It stands on a base surmounted by a cyma recta moulding. Admission is gained by a flight of steps flanked by plain side-walls.

The gateway measures 15' 6" square externally.

Ascending the spur, at whose foot these ruins are situated, we come to a very beautiful piece of open ground in the midst of dense forest. Among the trees at one corner of it are the scanty remains of the base of a small temple.

The long lines of walling between the temple and the village are regarded by tradition as the ruins of the old watch-station.

MANASBAL

One of the most attractive places in the valley is the Manasbal lake (Plate I). Being absolutely free from disturbance of any kind, and nestling in an oval basin surrounded on all sides by hills and uplands, the lake is an ideal abode for the happy lotus-eater, who dreams away his days reclining under the shady chinar, and passes his evenings in watching the long streaks of moonlight flitting across the mirror-like surface of the water. Naturally, such a delightful spot would not have been overlooked either by the devout Hindu or the nature-adoring Mughal. The former have left a small temple, now partially submerged during the greater part of the year. It is a very small structure, and only its two pyramidal roofs are visible in the driest seasons (Plate LXI).   The cornice of the lower roof, and the horizontal band which divides it from the upper storey, are decorated with series of dentils and metopes.   Only the upper part of the pediment of the entrance is visible.   It faces west.

A few yards from the temple, up the hill, is a natural cavern of no particular interest.   Further up is the Shahkul canal brought down from the Sindh river by Zain-ul-abidin.

On the south bank of the lake are ruins of a terraced Mughal garden, the construction of which is ascribed by tradition to Empress Nur Jahan.   The garden, locally known as the Jarogha, is entirely in ruins, the only parts standing being the retaining walls and the corner bastions of the terraces.

There are a number of sculptured stones, belonging to some Buddhist shrine, scattered about on top of the low ridge on the northern bank of the lake.

Andarkot

Near the entrance of the lake, on the left bank of the river, is the large village of Sumbal.   At a distance of a mile from it is situated Andarkot, known originally by the name of Jayapura, the capital of King Jayapida.   The site selected for the capital was in the midst of an extensive marsh, the drainage of which was so difficult a task that in Kalhana's time (twelfth century) it was believed that in the execution of his design the king had employed the services of *rakshasas*, " demons," whom his friend, King Vibhishana of Ceylon, had placed at his disposal.   The ancient causeway which connects the island with the mainland of Sumbal is still the only means of communication in the rainy season, when the lowlands round about are covered with water.

There is not much left today of the Buddhist *viharas* and Hindu temples which are said to have been built here by Jayapida. Practically everything has been destroyed.   The temple of Keśava

11

is represented by a large heap of scorched and shapeless boulders. The only objects of interest are a couple of sculptured reliefs on two faces of the pilaster of the stair; and they too are woefully defaced. The relief on the flank depicts a four-armed Vishnu seated on a cushioned throne in what is technically known as the *lalitasana* (sportive attitude), while an attendant, probably a female, is standing on his left. The left foot of the god rests upon a small footstool. His upper right hand holds a mace, and the lower one is placed in *abhayamudra* (pose of granting immunity from fear). He is profusely ornamented, and wears the *mandaramala* (garland of celestial flowers). Under his throne are an atlant and some other indistinct figures. The relief on the front panel contains a group of three figures: Vishnu seated between his two consorts.

The sculptures belong to about the seventh or eighth century A.D.

Andarkot has a particularly sorrowful interest for the Hindus of Kashmir, for it was in the fort here that the last Hindu ruler, Queen Kotadevi, surrendered to her rebellious servant, Shah Mir, on certain stipulations which he did not fulfil afterwards.

THE WULAR LAKE

The ancient name of the Wular lake was the Mahapadmasaras, (lake of Mahapadma), the great Serpent Deity. Its modern name is probably derived from the Sanskrit *ullola*, the lake with the " high-leaping " waves.

The historian Jonaraja states that King Zain-ul-abidin was anxious to build such a monument to his fame as had never been built by any king before. After much deliberation he decided to construct an island-palace in the middle of the Wular lake, but he was so greatly impressed with the magnitude of the task that he sought the wise men of his time for advice regarding the ways and means of its accomplishment. They encouraged his efforts by narrating the following legend:

In ancient times there was a city at that very place where there is the lake nowadays. The city was presided over by the great snake deity, Mahapadma. But the lapse of time, and the security given by beneficent rule, brought in its train luxury and vice among the citizens, which grew with such alarming rapidity that Mahapadma resolved upon the destruction of the entire city, including its inhabitants. But, among the residents of the doomed city was a humble and virtuous potter, whom the deity resolved to spare. He appeared to him in a dream and, warning him of the impending fate of the city, told him to save himself. Next morning the potter related the warning to the citizens, but was laughed at for his pains. As soon, therefore, as the potter left the city, the waters began to rise until the entire countryside was overwhelmed by one tremendous deluge. To quote from Jonaraja: "The terrified children who stood, at first when the water was low, at the feet of their mothers, soon, as the water began to rise higher, got into their laps, then clung to their breasts, next jumped upon their shoulders, and finally sat upon their heads, as if they were their embodied vital breaths. The flood covered the quaking limbs of women as if it were an affectionate lover embracing his beloved whose limbs are trembling with emotion."

After the Naga had thus wreaked his vengeance upon the sinful city, he established his permanent residence in the newly formed lake.

"The Lord of the Snakes was in reality Kaliya, who, being trampled upon by the feet of Krishna, bore the mark of a lotus on his head, and from that time onwards bore the appellation of Mahapadma."

Zain-ul-abidin's wise men then wound up their story by the naïve assurance that he, being an incarnation of Hari, could do as he pleased in the domain of his liege subject Mahapadma, and that his efforts would assuredly be crowned with success. He therefore set about vigorously for accomplishment of his purpose. Large cargo boats, which are still plentiful in Kashmir, were filled with boulders and sunk at the spot selected. The island was named Zainalanka after its builder, and still retains that name. The king built a small but very beautiful mosque at one corner of it, the ruins of which are still in existence. It is built of large blocks of limestone, similar to those used in the mediæval temples of Kashmir. Even the mouldings are those which are so common in the ancient Hindu temples. The principal decorative feature externally is a double row of trefoiled niches, which are flanked by pretty fluted columns surmounted by ribbed capitals. The lower row of niches stands on a quirked ovolo course, and is surmounted by a filleted torus. The corner pilasters have square filleted capitals. The two flank walls of the porch survive.

The interior was paved with large stone flags. The floor was on a level with the filleted torus outside.

A large assortment of architectural fragments of Hindu temples, such as fluted columns, stones from pilasters, jambs, etc., are scattered round about the site, which tends to prove that there was once a Hindu temple also on the island. This hypothesis is further strengthened by the presence of a big Śiva-linga, which is partly submerged, on the east side of the island. It is probable that the temple also was built by Zain-ul-abidin, for none of his successors on the Kashmir throne was capable of such a colossal task. There are indications to show that there were series of steps on all sides leading down to the water, though the principal landing seems to have been on the east side.

The only other structure on the island is a small domed chamber of brick masonry measuring 15' 7" square internally. This was also partly built of Hindu materials. The string-courses on top of the walls consist of projecting wooden beams. The entire surface of the chamber seems to have been coated with painted plaster. Externally the walls were adorned with shallow arched recesses which were originally covered with plaster. They were separated by glazed tiles. The square impressions of these tiles are visible on the plaster backing wherever it still adheres to the walls.   Fragments of painted and glazed tiles are lying in the debris.

The structure seems to be a tomb, and is probably contemporary with the mosque.

In 1874, Dr. Vincent Smith discovered on this island a stone slab bearing a Persian inscription which mentioned the name of Zain-ul-abidin and contained the date A.H. 847 = A.D. 1442-43.

Garur

On the north-eastern shore of the lake is situated the village of Garur.   It contains a small mediæval temple 4' 2" square internally, and 7' 3" high from basement to cornice.   The roof has disappeared and the base is buried underground.   The temple faces north-west and stands on the bank of a spring.   The steps which led down to the water are now missing.   The absence of the external trefoil niches is remarkable.   The roof was undoubtedly pedimented. There is a small pointed niche in each of these walls, which contains a sculptured relief.   That on the back bears a three-headed Śiva. The other two figures are too defaced to be identified with anything approaching certainty.

The ceiling is built of overlapping stones.

Wangath

The Srinagar-Sonamarg high road[1] branches off at Wusan to the mountain village of Wangath and the long and narrow glen known to sportsmen by the name of Wangath Nala.   The dense dark green forests of pine and fir which clothe the steep and in some places almost vertical hill-sides are favourite haunts of the bear in early autumn, when maize begins to ripen.   The cow-track—for the Wangath road is

---

[1] The traveller from Sonamarg will find it much more convenient to start from Kangan, where there is a dak bangalow.   The distance from here to Narannag is about 20 miles.   The road is practicable for ponies, but walking is more pleasant.   Tents and necessaries must be taken.   No shelter of any kind is available there.

nothing better—winds along the mountain spurs, always following the tortuous course of the Kanka-nadi torrent, whose white and foaming waters form a striking contrast to the sombre hue of the surrounding woods. On all sides the view is bounded by long ranges of hills rising higher and still higher as they recede until they terminate in the bare, jagged, towering peaks of Tilail. An uphill trudge of eight or nine miles brings the jaded traveller to Narannag, the site of an interesting group of temples which are commonly known as the Wangath temples, though the village bearing the name "Wangath" is three miles distant. They are situated at the foot of the Butsher mountain, whose extreme steepness and slipperiness have become proverbial, and have made it the terror and despair of Gangabal pilgrims.

Narannag is the modern name of ancient Sodaratirtha, which has been, since very early times, an important place of pilgrimage in Kashmir. The site probably owes its sanctity to the existence of a large spring, near which have been built two groups of temples belonging to the mediæval era. All the temples are more or less in ruins, chiefly owing to the inroads of vegetation. The stone used is the greyish granite which is found in abundance at the place. The first group, that is the one nearer Wangath, comprises six temples situated within an enclosure wall. Judging by their positions, as they are by no means symmetrically disposed in relation to one another, and by the difference in their architectural details, it is probable that the various structures were built at different dates (Plate LXII).

(1) The principal temple is a square of 25′, and, except in a few particulars, does not differ from other temples of Kashmir. The first point of departure from the usual style are the entrances. We have seen the temples of the *vimana* type, which have all the four sides open. But this one has two entrances opposite each other in the north-east and south-west sides. The second distinction is its domed ceiling, though there is no doubt that externally the roof was pyramidal. A large quantity of lime has been used in the masonry of the temple. The ceiling is built of circular courses of *kanjur* stone, and is crowned at the

apex by a full-blown lotus. The dome springs from four large corner stones, which cut off the angles formed by the walls. On two sides of the string-course upon which the dome rests are eight rectangular slots (four on each side), which seem to have been intended to hold the rafters of a canopy over the image. The interior measures 17' square. In the centre of the floor is a square space which is unpaved. It marks the site of the pedestal of the image. The mortices of the tenons of the doors can still be seen in both entrances.

The two sides which are closed are decorated externally with square-topped recesses, each of which contains the pedestal of an image which was probably a replica of the one in the sanctum itself. The core of the roof consists of rubble-stone masonry in lime.

This temple has been identified by Sir Aurel Stein with the Jyeshtheśa temple of Lalitaditya.

(2) The small temple to the left possesses niches on three sides intended for images. Their pedestals with tenons are *in situ*. Part of the *kanjur* backing of the dome is intact on top of the walls.

(3) The temple immediately touching the porch of the preceding shrine is a single square structure, plain both internally and externally. One stone of the roof, which is the only one *in situ*, shows that the ceiling was not domical, but was built of overlapping stones. (4) Immediately behind is the basement of another small temple. Its superstructure has fallen down. (5-6) Of the two temples behind, one has its entrance facing north-east, and the other faces south-east. The ceiling of the former was of the overlapping type while that of the latter was probably domical. (7) Immediately to the left of the latter is the ruined plinth of another temple, smaller than any of those described above.

The gateway of the enclosure is situated, curiously enough, at the north-west corner, and not in the middle of the wall, as is the case in other temples. It is, as usual, a two-chambered structure. In each chamber are the bases of two columns which supported the roof of the porch. Fragments of circular columns which stood on the bases are lying strewn round about the site. The retaining wall of the plinth on which this group of temples stands is built of closely packed pieces of slate, and in places where vegetation has not played havoc with it, it is very compact and beautiful.

A broad causeway paved with huge blocks of granite leads to the second group of temples, situated about two hundred yards farther off.

Between the two groups of temples are a number of structures which in themselves deserve to be classed into a third group. All of them have fallen down, but one, the base only of which is in existence, is unique in Kashmir. It appears to have been a spacious pillared hall or *barahdari* about 100' long by 67' broad. The bases of the columns are *in situ*. They are eight in number on the longer side and four on the shorter. The staircase is built between the central pair of columns facing the first group of temples. The slots in the landing on the top of the stairs seem to have been intended for holding the posts of screens.

The lower group of temples is likewise enclosed in a massive rectangular stone wall pierced by a two-chambered gateway. Inside the wall are half a dozen structures, all in ruined condition and partly buried under the ground. The largest temple has been identified by Sir Aurel Stein with that of Śiva-Bhuteśvara.[1] Internally it is a square of 17', and was similar to the largest temple in the first group. The small temple to its right has a round-headed entrance. There are two small shrines on its south, the first of which differs from all the structures at this site in that it is built of small pieces of slate in lime mortar, placed upon a granite base.[2] The peculiar feature of the second is an immense rectangular stone trough carved out of a single gigantic block of granite. Among the objects lying scattered about the compound, the most noteworthy

[1] *Rajat.*, v, 55, note.
[2] In this characteristic it resembles the subsidiary shrines in the courtyard of the Bandi temple. See p. 159.

are two fragments, in the south-east corner of the quadrangle, of an octagonal pedestal of a Śiva-linga, and two stones in the same corner of the quadrangle, each decorated with a pair of remarkably well-executed geese.

The long raised line of brick masonry on the enclosure wall is the debris of the cellular quadrangle which usually surrounds the Kashmiri temple.

Outside the north-western corner of the peristyle is the large spring, the real lodestone of the pilgrims, which was the occasion of all this magnificence.   Its cool, delicious water, perhaps, contributed to some extent to its sanctity.   The water issues out of the mountain side through the masonry walls of the tank.   Slightly higher up, and more than half-buried under the ground, is a small temple whose double pyramidal roof is the only existing roof in the whole group of temples here.   This has been identified by Sir Aurel Stein with the temple of Bhairava,[1] near which the turbulent baron Dhanva was decapitated for encroaching upon the lands and revenues of these temples.

Before leaving the site, the visitor should not fail to observe the unusually massive stone retaining wall of this group of temples. The granite blocks are of so extraordinary a size and are so beautifully dressed and finely joined as to give the impression that their carvers regarded them more in the light of wooden beams than as close-grained intractable boulders to be chipped into shape with vigilant care and inexhaustible patience.   It is probable that this wall served the double purpose of protecting the temple enclosure from being overwhelmed by the debris of the hill above, and also as the back wall of the range of cells on this side.   The site has from time immemorial enjoyed a very high degree of popular esteem, which remains unimpaired to this day, thanks to the pilgrims who, after consigning the ashes of their dead relatives to the Gangabal lake, make it a point to offer worship here.   The temples were endowed

---

[1] Rajat., v, 55-59.

with extensive estates, and the priests in charge seem to have been a particularly influential body.   In the later mediæval period, after the death of Avantivarman, these temples shared the misfortunes which came upon Kashmir with ever-increasing violence.   The temple treasury was plundered by Bhadreśvara, the minister of Samgramaraja (A.D. 1003-1028); a conflagration in the reign of Uchchala (A.D. 1101-1111) inflicted much damage upon the buildings; during the reign of Jayasimha (A.D. 1128-1155), Hayavadana, a rebel baron, had the temples " sacked by marauding hillmen."   Sumanas, a brother of Rilhana, the minister of Jayasimha, built a *matha* or congregation hall here.   It is possible that the pillared hall is this same *matha*.   Further excavations may throw light upon the question.

SHORT BIBLIOGRAPHY ON THE HISTORY AND ARCHÆOLOGY OF KASHMIR

ABUL FAZL. *Ain-i-Akbari.*   Translated by Blochmann and Jarrett.

ABUL FAZL. *Akbarnama.*   Translated by Beveridge.

ALBERUNI. *India.*   Translated by E. Sachau.

BEAL, SAMUEL. *Life of Hiuen Tsiang.*

BERNIER, FRANÇOIS. *Travels in the Mughal Empire.*

BUHLER, GEORG.   Report of a tour in search of MSS.   *J.B.B.R.A.S.*

CATROU. *General History of the Mughal Empire.*

COLE, LIEUTENANT H. *Kashmir Monuments.*

COWIE, Rev. W. G. Notes on some of the Temples of Kashmir in the *J.A.S.B.*   1866.

CUNNINGHAM, SIR ALEXANDER. Essay on the Arian Order of Architecture in the *J.A.S.B.*   1848.

CUNNINGHAM, SIR ALEXANDER. *Ancient Geography of India.*

DREW, F. *Jammu and Kashmir Territories.*

DUTT, J. C. *Kings of Kashmir,* vol. iii.

ELLIOT, SIR H. M. *History of India by its own Historians.*   8 vols.

ELPHINSTONE, MOUNTSTUART. *History of India.*

FERGUSSON, JAMES. *History of Indian and Eastern Architecture.*

FERISHTA. *History of India.*   Translated by Colonel Briggs.

HAIG, COLONEL. *The Sultans of Kashmir,* in the *J.R.A.S.*   1918.

KALHANA. *Rajatarangini.*   Translated by Sir Aurel Stein.

LATIF, SYED MUHAMMAD. *History of the Punjab.*

LAWRENCE, SIR WALTER. *Valley of Kashmir.*

MANUCCI, NICOLAO. *Storia do Mogor.*   1908.

MARSHALL, SIR JOHN. *Note on Archæological Work in Kashmir.*

MIRZA HAIDAR. *Tarikh-i-Rashidi,* by Mirza Haider Doghlat of Kashgar.   Translated by Elias and Ross.

NICHOLLS, J. H. *Mughal Gardens of Kashmir.*

NICHOLLS, J. H. *Muhammadan Architecture of Kashmir.*   *A.S.R.*   1906-07.

PANIKKAR, K. M. *Gulab Singh.*

SAHNI, DAYA RAM, R. B. *Pre-Muhammadan Monuments of Kashmir,* in the *A.S.R.* for 1915-16.   *Avantipur temples, Ibid.,* 1912.

SI-YU-KI. *The Buddhist Records of the Western World.* Translated by Beal.

SMITH, V. A. *Early History of India.*

STEIN, SIR AUREL, *Notes on the Pir Panjal Route. Notes on the Itinerary of Oukong.* Translation of the *Rajatarangini* of Kalhana.

STUART, MRS. C. M. VILLIERS. *Gardens of the Great Mughals.*

Treaties, Sanads and Engagements of India, by Aitchison, vol. xi.

TUZUK-I-JAHANGIRI. Translated by Rogers and Beveridge.

WATTERS, THOMAS. *On Yuan Chwang's Travels in India.*

Readers may also consult the travels of Forster, Moorcroft, Honigberger, Hügel, Jacquemont and Vigne.

Among the unpublished sources, the principal are the Persian Histories of Kashmir by Haidar Malik, Hasan, Narayan Kaul and Birbal Katsar.

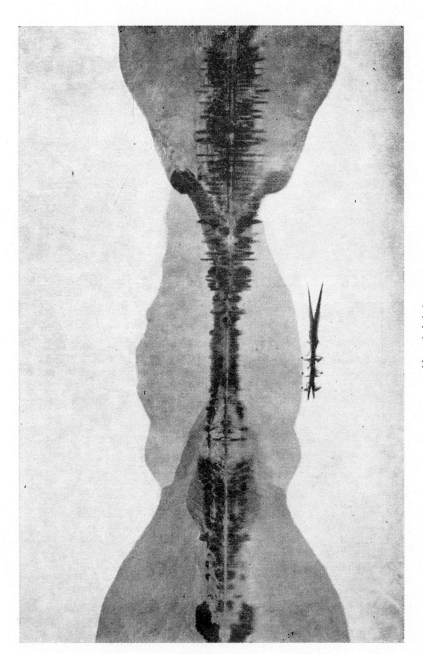

Manasbal. Lake.

Pahalgam Valley.

Picking Saffron at Pampur.

IV

Sankaracharya (Takht-i-Sulaiman) Hill.

Sankaracharya Temple.

Khanqah of Shah Hamadan.

Patthar Masjid.

VIII

Mausoleum of Zain-ul-Abidin's Mother.

Jama' Masjid.

Jama' Masjid : Spire of a Minar.

Hari Parbat Hill, Fort, and Rampart.

Mosque of Akhun Mulla Shah.

Nishat Bagh.

Shalimar Bagh : Marble Pavilion and Fountains.

Harwan : General View of Excavations ; Lower Terrace.

Harwan : Triple Base of Stupa in Diaper-Rubble Style.

Harwan : Fragment of Wall in Pebble Style.

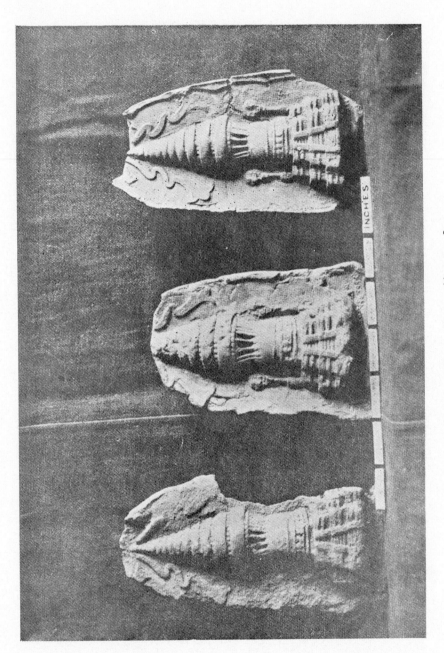

Harwan : Terracotta Plaques Showing Miniature Stupas.

Harwan : Wall of Apsidal Temple   in Diaper-Pebble Style with Portion of Tile-Pavement.

Harwan : Closer view of tile-Pavement in situ.

Harwan : Tile-Covered Courtyard and Platform.

XXII

2.

Above: men and women seated in a balcony. The workmanship of these figures is remarkably delicate and the features are better delineated than in the preceding group. Middle: three ascetics in the "kakasana"—i.e., "crow posture." Below: geese holding stalks of half-blown lotuses in their bills. Kharoshthi numerals: 20, 20, I = 41.

1.

Above: a row of conventional cocks in medallions. Below: two pairs of men and women facing each other in a balcony.

4.

Above : floral scroll. Below : man and woman, evidently from the same mould as those to left.
Kharoshthi numerals: 1, 1, 1, 4, 10 = 17.

3.

Above : man and woman facing each other, seated in a balcony.
The man holds in his left hand a lotus bud. The coarse
features, low receding forehead, high cheek-bones, and
prominent noses of both man and woman are noteworthy.
Below: on a horse fully accoutred, horseman in armour
riding at full gallop and drawing his bow. On his right
side, attached to the saddle, hangs his quiver. Two ends
of drapery flutter at his back. Kharoshthi numerals:
1, 4, 10 = 15.

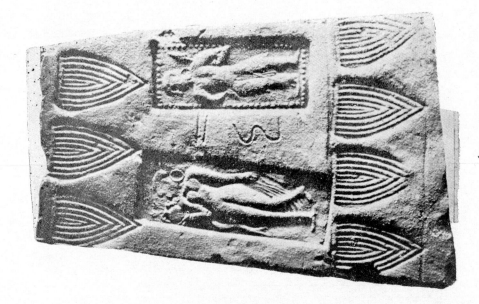

5.

Female figure in transparent robe advances to left, holding vase of flowers on upraised right hand and lifting skirt with left hand. She wears a kind of close-fitting turban and large ear-rings. On three sides, procession of geese with uplifted wings; lotus-petal band below. Kharoshthi numerals: 10, 4, I = 15.

6.

Left: female figure as in (5). Right: standing soldier (Amazon?) with spear, within pearl border. Above and below: rows of aquatic leaves or lotus petals, Kharoshthi numerals: I, I, 20 = 22.

8.

Left : water-carrier, realistically drawn, carrying two water-pots. Right: female wearing thin robe and stole, carries flower vase or incense-burner on up-raised left hand and supports skirt with right. Kharoshthi numerals : 1, 10, 20 = 32.

7.

Segmental tile with projecting lower rim. Above : the same figure as on (5), repeated. Below : pair of figures in balcony, conversing; repeated three and a half times. Part of lower edge broken away. (Tiles 5, 6 and 7 are glazed. They show delicate modelling and appear to be of earlier date than those previously described.)

10.

Segmental tile. Above: two putti supporting a heavy floral festoon. Below: cock with foliate tail within a circle, repeated; upside down. Kharoshthi numerals: 10, 4, 1, 1, 1 (inverted) = 17.

9.

Segmental tile. Above: row of aquatic leaves. Below: two youthful figures (putti) supporting a heavy floral festoon. Kharoshthi numerals: 1, 4 = 5.

12.

A dancer wearing large ear-rings and dressed in loose robe and trousers, with a long scarf held in both hands, which she waves over her head.

11.

Above : row of lotus medallions. Below : female musician wearing trousers; she plays on a drum, which is apparently slung over her left shoulder. Floral motifs on either side.

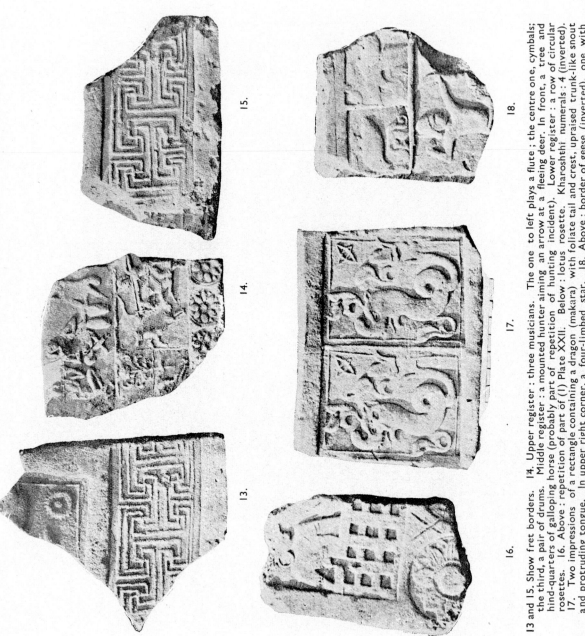

13 and 15. Show fret borders.   14. Upper register : three musicians.   The one to left plays a flute ; the centre one, cymbals; the third, a pair of drums.   Middle register : a mounted hunter aiming an arrow at a fleeing deer. In front, a tree and hind-quarters of galloping horse (probably part of repetition of hunting incident).   Lower register : a row of circular rosettes. 16. Above : repetition of part of (1) Plate XXII.   Below : lotus rosette.   Kharoshthi numerals : 4 (inverted).   17.   Two impressions of a rectangle containing a dragon (makara) with foliate tail and crest, upraised trunk-like snout and protruding tongue. In upper right corner, a four-limbed star. 18. Above : border of geese (inverted), one with

19.

Above : a conventional rosette.   Below : a row of galloping
stags and rosettes.

20.

Above : lotus medallions.   Below : to left, a running stag with great
antlers, and rosettes in front and rear, as in 19.   To right a
huntsman with bow and arrow riding at full gallop.   Just in
front of him is part of another panel, which must have contained a stag similar to the one on the left.   Kharoshthi
numerals : 1, 4, 20, 20, 20= 65.

22.

In central circle, a cock, regardant, with foliate tail; surrounded by circle of roundels; the whole within rectangular frame of pearls.

21.

Above: left, conventional fleur-de-lis. Centre, rosettes. Right, circular flower vase on a tripod. Below: cocks fighting over what appears to be a lily bud.

23.
Part of border moulding with enclosed palmette and hatching.

24.
Fragment of medallion. Youthful figure surrounded by
flowers.

25.
Above : row of aquatic leaves. Below : combat between
a griffin and a man holding a heavy-headed mace.
Between the two is a wheel over which the two
appear to be fighting.

26.
Above : cow suckling a calf, realistically drawn; repeated· Below.
floral scroll. Kharoshthi numerals: 4, 10, 20 = 34.

27.
Above: cows and calves.   Below: a row of fleur-de-lis.
Kharoshthi numerals: 1, 1, 1 = 3.

29.
Roughly executed vase with flowers, on stepped base. (Cf. 28.)

28.
Above : medallion containing conventional foliate bird; repeated. Below: globular vase on moulded foot, containing lily-like flowers; repeated. Kharoshthi numerals:
l, l, l = 3.

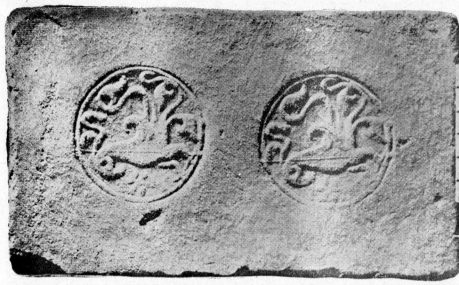

31.

Medallion containing conventional cock with foliated tail ; repeated.

30.

Above: conventional fleur-de-lis with stems encircled by ring; repeated. Below: the same, reversed. Centre: full-blown lotus; repeated. Kharoshthi numerals: 1, 1, 10, 20, 20 = 53.

33.

Above: geese running and flapping their wings, with scarves in their bills. Second: rows of lotus petals cut at the base, with points directed outwards. Third: floral pattern with bunches of grapes. Below: row of lotus petals cut at the bases. Kharoshthi numerals: I, I, 20, 20 = 42.

32.

Segmental tile. Above: conventional fleur-de-lis as 30; repeated. Centre: a motif consisting of an aquatic leaf standing on the pod of an aquatic fruit (juwar) common in Kashmir. Below: two lotus medallions. Kharoshthi numerals: 4, I, I = 6.

34.
Architectural moulding. Right: lotus
petals. Left: grape-vine scroll.
(Cf. 33.)

35.
Architectural moulding. Right: fleur-de-
lis. Left: rosette.

37. Full-blown lotus surrounded by eight whirling rosettes (or suns) and four aquatic leaves or lotus petals pointing to the four corners of rectangular tile.

36. Full-blown lotus surrounded by eight radiating aquatic leaves or lotus petals. Kharoshthi numerals: I, I, I ⹀ 3.

Below : a full-blown lotus from which rises a stem supporting three aquatic leaves,

38.

A bunch of seven lotus buds with cincture round stems.

41.
Above : cocks fighting. (Cf. 21.) Below: leaves with long stems. Kharoshthi numerals: 4, 4 = 8.

40.
Below: a row of elephants in a lotus garden; one elephant is placed upside down, perhaps owing to error in the stamping of the mould. From the flower garden spring what appear to be aquatic leaves with long stems. Kharoshthi numerals: (perhaps) 1, 10, 20, 20 = 51, inverted.

43: Rosette surrounded by circle of sunk dots and lines within

42. Full-blown lotus surrounded by circle of pearls within

45.
Rosette with cock regardant in centre. " Herring-bone "
border. Kharoshthi numerals: 1, 10 = 12.

44.
Rosette.

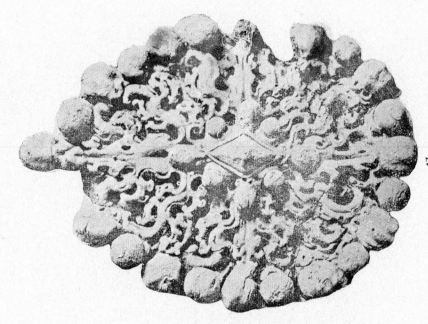

47.
Terracotta pendant from necklace of colossal figure of a
Bodhisattva.

46,
Fret border and lotus petals.

Yandrahom Megaliths.

Pandrethan Temple.

Bodhisattva Discovered at Pandrethan.

Mosque at Pampur.

Temple at Loduv.

Avantisvami Temple : General view from the rear.

Avantisvami Temple : General View from the Front.

Avantisvami Temple : Relief on Pilaster of Stair.

Payar Temple.

Temple at Narastan.

Martand Temple : General View.

Vernag Spring.

Basement of Stupa at Parihasapura.

Sankaragaurisvara Temple at Patan.

Miniature Temple at Patan.

Terracotta Heads Discovered at Ushkar.

PLATE LIX

Siva Linga at Baramula.

Buniar Temple.

Submerged Temple in the Manasbal Lake.

Wangath Temples.

LXIII

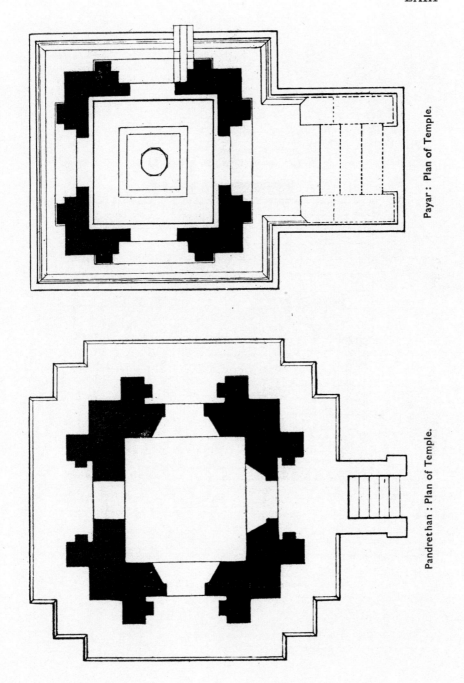

Payar : Plan of Temple.

Pandrethan : Plan of Temple.

Pandrethan : Elevation of Temple.

Pandrethan : Section Through Temple.

Pandrethan : Detail of Temple Ceiling.

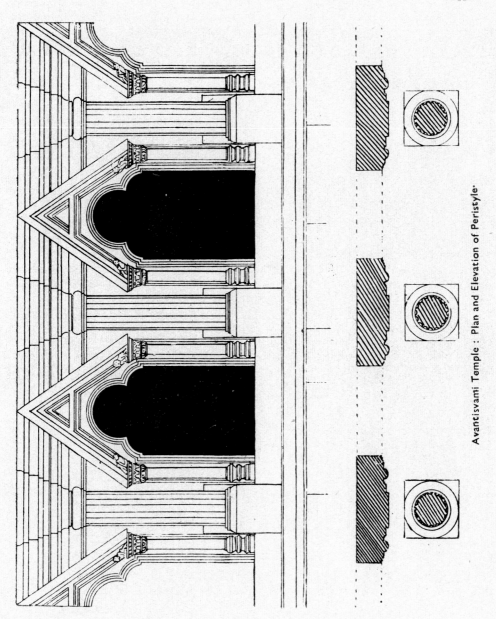

Avantisvami Temple : Plan and Elevation of Peristyle.

LXX

(A) AVANTISVAMI TEMPLE : KIRTIMUKHA CORNICE.

(B) Avantisvami Temple : Section and Elevation of Plinth.

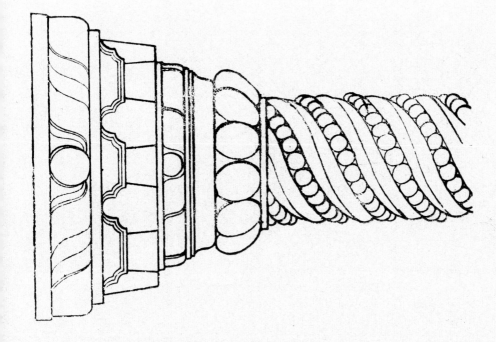

AVANTISVAMI TEMPLE : DETAIL OF COLUMNS OF PERISTYLE

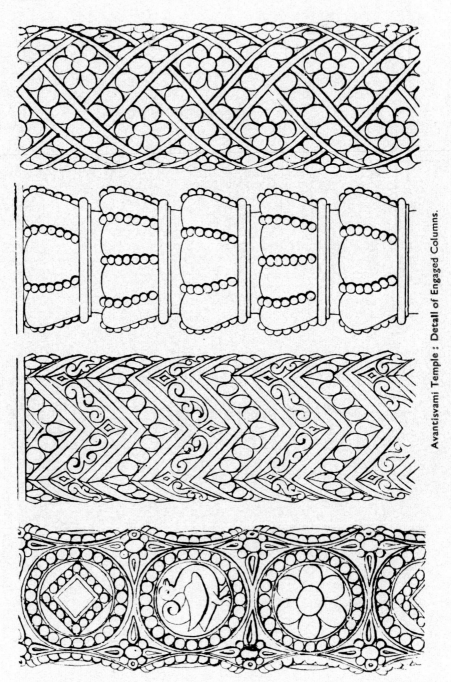

Avantisvami Temple : Detail of Engaged Columns.

MARTAND : PLAN OF TEMPLE.

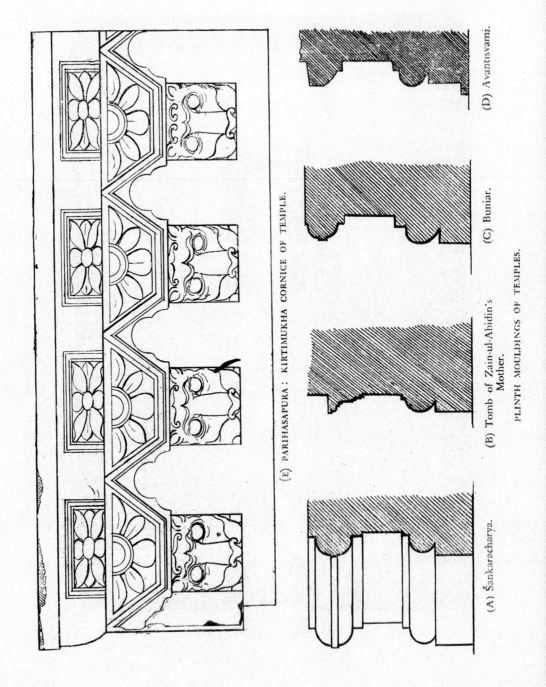

(E) PARIHASAPURA : KIRTIMUKHA CORNICE OF TEMPLE.

(A) Śankaracharya.

(B) Tomb of Zain-ul-Abidin's Mother.

(C) Buniar.

(D) Avantsvami.

PLINTH MOULDINGS OF TEMPLES.

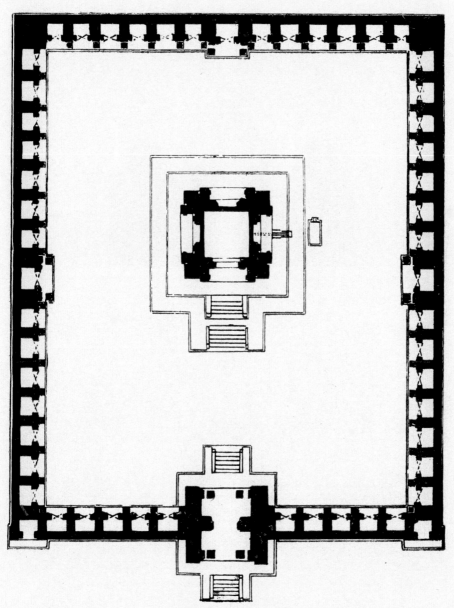

Buniar : Plan of Temple.

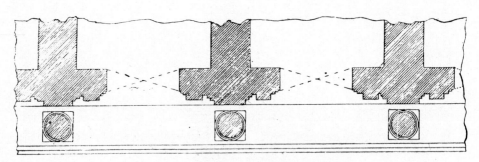

Buniar : Plan and Elevation of Temple Peristyle.

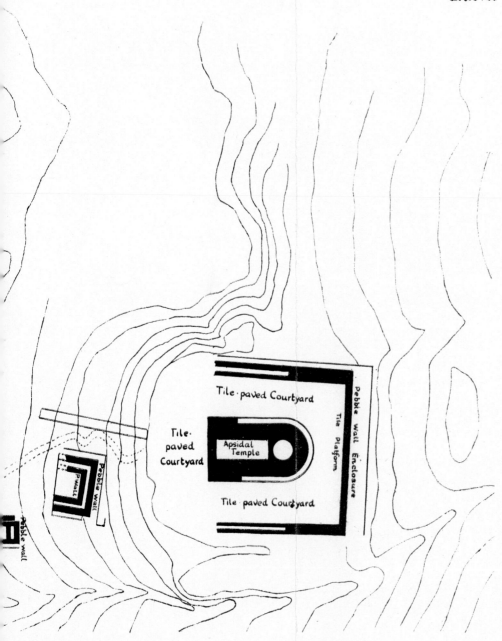

Tile-paved Courtyard

Tile-paved Courtyard

Tile-paved Courtyard

Tile-paved Courtyard

Apsidal Temple

Pebble Wall Enclosure

Tile Platform

Pebble wall

Pebble wall

Pebble wall

of Excavations.

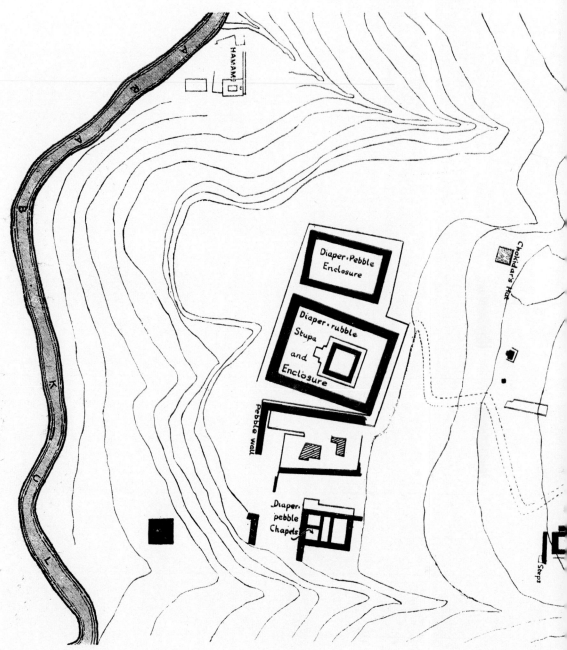

Harwan : General Site-Plan

28 D